Qwest for Truth ...and Change

Rick Weston

Qwest for Truth...and Change

Weston, Rick @2017

All Rights Reserved: No part of this publication may be reproduced, stored in a retrieval system or transmitted in any form or by any means—electronic, mechanical, photocopying, recording or otherwise—without the prior written permission of the author.

Library of Congress Cataloging-in-Publishing Data

I. Business studies   II. Corporate Culture

III. Memoir—Business

HF 5351 W 2017   383.7W

ISBN: 978-0-9906120-0-1

Printed in the United States of America

table of contents

ONE	Qwest for Truth....and Change	7
TWO	My personal journey	10
THREE	Enter the wireless revolution	25
FOUR	Certain Transactions...and COBRAs...Be Wary of Their Bite	42
FIVE	Genuity—the real deal, having genuine character (Urban Dictionary)	50
SIX	Can I call you Joe?	55
SEVEN	Philip F. Anschutz—the man with the Midas touch...	68
EIGHT	Corporate Culture	76
NINE	Qwest Communications International Inc.	98
TEN	And Change...	118
	About the Author	141

dedication

THIS BOOK IS A TRIBUTE *to all of the terrific people
I had the opportunity to work with over the years
and learn so much from as we rode the wave.*

*Special thanks are given to the two
most influential managers in my career,
Bob Philpot and Rich Burk.*

*Also, this is dedicated to my children,
Aaron and Erica, of whom I am so proud
as they continue growing in their careers,
and for their mother who stood by me
when others did not.*

*Finally, this is for the light of my life, Jo,
who provided the inspiration
to complete this work.*

ONE
qwest for truth…and change

ACCORDING TO MARK TWAIN, "If you tell the truth, you don't have to remember anything."

I know what you must be thinking, why write a book about a company that no longer exists? I am writing this book for several reasons: First, I don't believe the story has ever been told as to what actually transpired within the company. The accounting has never been litigated, and it won't be here. However, it will be discussed. Second, and most importantly, what does the story of Qwest teach us? Have we put any of these lessons to work in the decade that has ensued since the company's legal issues arose?

Qwest is now Century Link, Inc. The company is not in the headlines any longer, and its history as Qwest is remembered by scandal, including SEC investigations, criminal indictments, and the incarceration of its former Chief Executive Joseph Nacchio, as well as the loss of shareowner and employee wealth.

A good amount of time has passed, but there is still a great deal we can learn from the Qwest experience. It is important that we do so because we seem to be on a path where we are either repeating some of the same mistakes, or, in some cases, over reacting.

My intent is to describe what happened inside of the company, and what happened to me. You can then make your own determinations about events and the resulting changes in regulation, legislation, and management practices that could prevent the destruction of another company and loss of wealth.

In these pages, I also explore that amorphous but essential element known as "corporate culture." I hope to identify some of the root cause issues that occurred in this business and examine the role of individuals within the company.

How we interacted with management; actions we took to reach the goals set in the business; and the efforts by management to meet the expectations of institutional investors, analysts, the business media, and shareowners are examined.

Along with this particular corporate scandal, those of Bernard Madoff and R. Alan Stanford are addressed. The SEC has grown significantly since the time of Qwest, but they still did not catch the Ponzi schemes of Bernard Madoff or R. Alan Stanford, despite innumerable indications, clues, evidence, and individuals pleading with the agency to act. The SEC failed the investing public. This is not to say I have absolute disdain for the SEC, as I do understand their mission and role in protecting investors. I do believe that, like all bureaucracies, they can lose focus and become enraptured by those they are supposed to be regulating. I do not harbor ill will, despite the damage their actions have had on me; but they need to change, and all evidence in the ensuing decade suggests that change comes slowly.

Of further relevance is understanding the role incentives play in corporate America. Many employees have experienced how important these incentives are, as well as the law of unintended consequences in the financial system meltdown that led to the Great Recession. The result was extraordinary measures taken not only by the Federal Reserve but the administrations of George W. Bush and Barack Obama as well.

THIS BOOK is my attempt to make lemonade out of lemons and to turn what has been a horrible experience for me personally into something positive. In what follows, I hope to initiate a discussion for change to be considered by executives, managers, regulators, and individual employees. My intention is that this book will allow us to look at what happened at Qwest and discuss some ideas that can enable us to avoid circumstances that destroy companies, put people in jail, ruin careers and reputations, and lead to the destruction of economic value.

In this discussion, I will also briefly explore the other accounting scandals of the time and how effective those additional regulations are in response to those events. This is an examination of what happened at Qwest a decade ago, but more importantly, has anything changed? Have we changed the root causes?

I hope you enjoy the journey with me.

TWO
my personal journey

MY FATHER WAS a career military officer who served in the Air Force for 30 years. He was a brilliant, yet volatile, man. He could be quite mean. Over time, we became close; I think it was the birth of my two children that calmed the waters. I was certainly proud of his accomplishments and felt that confronting him on his past behavior would serve no purpose. We made our peace.

My mother was a homemaker and very funny. She was the life of the party. Unfortunately, her lifestyle of drinking, smoking, and being overweight claimed her far too soon. She was a life master bridge player and became an accomplished (at least by my standards) painter later in life.

I have two older brothers; both are retired now: one from PG&E, the other from the Postal Service. I have a younger sister who is a dental hygienist.

Despite being a military family, we did not move much. I was born at Mt. Home AFB in Idaho. I spent time in New York when my father was in England. When I was in second grade, we moved from Riverside, CA (March AFB) to Merced, CA (Castle AFB). As a sophomore in high school, we moved to Grand Forks AFB in North Dakota. (My father obviously made someone angry to get that plum assignment.) My father, then a colonel, retired from the Air Force after that tour. We returned to Merced where he bought a business where my parents worked. The opportunity to acquire the business arose after a race riot at the high school. A principle target was the son of the business' owner. The owner decided to move to another town because of the riots. I will also mention there were severe racial tensions and riots at the base in Grand Forks. This was 1972.

I was in my senior year in high school when we returned to Merced. I found myself uninterested in school and more interested in a girl. Unfortunately, I was expelled for truancy. I was also kicked out of my family's home at the same time. Being a decent student academically was not enough. There was just too much tension at school and home. I eventually completed my high school education at a continuation school and went on to attend Merced Community College. I found that I wasn't really interested in school and left after stints playing on the golf team and being a DJ at the college's radio station. In order to make enough money to live and play golf, I began working in the restaurant business. I also joined a hard rock band (playing bass guitar), produced another band, and staged a couple of concerts. I also spent a year as a ski bum during one of the drought years in California.

In time, I began to feel this was not what I wanted out of life, particularly after tending bar and watching drunks make fools of themselves and get violent. In the end, waiting on the "drunk and hungry" for handouts led me in a different direction, thankfully. Also during this time, I reconnected with a girl I knew and was enamored with prior to my sojourn to the frozen tundra of the

Dakotas. She was a nice girl and I thought an excellent choice to settle down with. We got married in Merced and immediately moved to Sacramento where I enrolled in school at California State University. Kristine, my then wife, was employed by Pacific Telephone. She transferred to Sacramento and enrolled in night school at the same university to complete her degree.

My academic interest was in public administration, with some business and computer science. My career goal upon graduating was employment in a government agency and perhaps later to pursue a career in politics. Hey, I was young and (foolishly) idealistic.

I put myself through school by working in restaurants. Tuition was relatively inexpensive in those times, except for the cost of books. My mother helped out by paying for my parking pass.

One of the requirements to graduate was to perform an internship. I was fortunate to have a professor who had many connections, and I was able to get an unpaid intern role at California's State Personnel Department. The task was to help them get their job classifications updated in the data centers operated by the state. I was told California operated the largest data centers west of the Mississippi River. These Included: Health and Welfare, Motor Vehicles, Franchise Tax Board, Board of Equalization, the Stephen P. Teale Data Center, and others. These data centers were large IBM mainframe environments located in Sacramento. There were a few Amdahl and other machines, but generally, it was all IBM.

The Personnel Department was wrestling with the specific job classifications of Applications Specialist, Operating System Specialist, and Hardware Analysts. I went to a number of the data centers and interviewed people in these job classifications. It became clear that to solve problems, they needed a universal position conversant with the interaction of those three major elements of the computing environment. It was a bit more involved than I portray here, but you have the essence.

The report input from the several of us working on the job was written in longhand and given to the secretarial pool (that is what it was called then). They returned the document after typing it into a Wang word processor. If you wanted to reorder your thoughts, you literally had to cut and paste (with scissors and glue) the sentences and words to their new position and then take them back to the typing pool. After months of this exercise, the document was complete, along with the recommendations the professional staff was making.

We went to the boss' office to present our findings. The room was spacious and had a conference table abutting his desk to form a large "T." While the office was fairly large, it seemed cramped, as there were books and large binders strewn about. The department head made the presentation of the findings to the boss and other associated stakeholders. I was proud of the work we had done and thought the recommendations would be beneficial to the employees and users of IT services. I asked as we departed, "What happens next?" He laughed and replied, "Did you see all those other binders in there collecting dust?" He then informed me, "… nothing ever moves in that office." So, that was that. *What a weird office environment,* I remember thinking. I thought we were doing serious work there, yet on Fridays, the staff went out to lunch for pizza and beer. A number of them took naps once back in the office. I decided right then that my government service career was over. I received help from the State of California since the funding for the project was terminated. I wanted my work to have greater meaning, relevance, and consequence.

That experience allowed me to check the internship box and graduate in May of 1983. In the months leading up to that point, I was thinking about my future and career opportunities. I applied at IBM, Johnson Wax, and AT&T. All of these blue-chip companies had renowned sales and management training programs. Perhaps this could make up for not attending a prestigious Ivy League or California school and getting an advanced degree.

My career begins with AT&T

I had developed an interest in technology companies after my introduction to the computer systems I used in college. My interest grew during the internship, as well as seeing large-scale operations and these massive raised-floor data centers.

I was looking to become a participant in what was clearly the future.

AT&T was interesting in that it had earlier agreed to end the government's antitrust litigation by agreeing to divest itself of the Bell Telephone operating companies. As a result of the breakup of the AT&T monopoly, the company would get its long-desired opportunity to take on IBM in the world of computing. To that end, AT&T launched its deregulated subsidiary in the year preceding the actual divestiture that occurred on January 1, 1984. The period was known as bifurcation, where the companies were to begin operating independently of one another. This period included: planning for the future, preparing to split assets, setting up rules for interaction, and the like. It was all very complex.

The deregulated subsidiary was launched as American Bell, Inc. and was responsible for the sale of telephone equipment in addition to the new line of computers the company was introducing. My then-wife was working on the equipment side of Pacific Telephone and was slated to transfer to American Bell, Inc. (ABI) on 1/1/84 as it was referred to. I met a number of her colleagues and others in the sales and services organizations. Frank McReynolds, whose job title was "Expeditor/Coordinator" (seriously), took an interest in me. He introduced me to Major Accounts Branch Manager Jim Hirschy. His administrative assistant, Doreen Lehr (and Frank's girlfriend), scheduled several interviews for me with him. I don't know why, but he apparently liked me and let me sit in his office at times and watch him work. He was on the phone, asking sales executives to give him updates on deals they were working, discussing tactics and contract terms. He had this nice office and a big desk; everything was new in the deregulated business. I was impressed.

After a month of "interviews," he finally told me he had no openings but would take me to the general business division where they might have something. I was introduced to a couple of sales managers and Branch Manager Charlie Massey. Mr. Massey was a silver-haired man who wore a navy blue pinstriped suit, crisp white shirt, and a yellow silk tie. I was very impressed. He was the person I wanted to be! I was offered the job as an account executive, selling telephone systems to small businesses. I did receive some sales and product training, and supplemented that with reading and going to sales seminars (e.g., Tom Hopkins and Zig Ziglar). Anyone who has been in sales knows it is very difficult and requires drive and discipline. You have to make a large number of sales calls, appointments, presentations, and proposals to have any chance. Time management is critical. Keeping your promises is crucial.

In 1983, business and economic conditions were not terrific. I concluded that professionals were my best target market and called on doctors and lawyers. As their time is valuable, I did plenty of sales calls after hours. I also discovered that many businesses were leasing equipment from AT&T. Much of the equipment was antiquated, and AT&T's current offerings were technically inferior to competitors. AT&T had invested in new technology for large businesses and introduced the System 85 (code named Antelope) that was very competitive. It would be a couple of months until we were able to sell the Merlin system (no code name), which was state of the art and designed for use by small businesses.

A year later, the medium-sized business system called System 75 (code named Gazelle) was introduced. (The names did not have much inspiration; the System 75 was later referred to as the Definity System 75. A vestige of being a monopoly?) It didn't take me long to realize this was a fiercely competitive market. AT&T could have sat back and milked its embedded base of rental revenues, but it wanted to compete. In this timeframe, AT&T introduced its 3B line of computers running UNIX (another great marketing name: 3B). These computing environments had been used in large scale across the telephone business, running signaling networks for call control, and advanced services such as 800 numbers and calling cards. When these machines were launched, we were told any customer considering an IBM System 36 or 38 should be offered the 3B. One small problem arose: the AT&T systems had no applications to run on them. (Seriously.) I recall us hustling to get a third-party application written for an electronic time card for payroll. One would have thought AT&T would be more prepared for its epic battle with IBM.

American Bell, Inc. was launched with great fanfare on New Year's Eve by sponsoring the ball drop in Times Square. American Bell was launched with $5.5 billion in seed capital, meant to last for five years until it was profitable. That seed money lasted only three and one-half years.

After the break-up occurred on January 1, 1984, I asked to be transferred to the long-distance and data unit that was renamed AT&T Communications (from AT&T Long Lines). This, the Major Accounts branch, had customers with annual telecom expenditures between $500,000 and $5 million. This revenue was comprised of a mix of private-line data services, long distance, 800 numbers, calling cards, and such. The group was relocated to downtown Sacramento in new office space. I was brought in as an Associate Account Executive.

This Major Accounts branch handled large local businesses and state government accounts, but no national accounts as there were no mega businesses headquartered in Sacramento. All of my colleagues were a product of the Bell System. They grew up in a monopoly and were now facing an onslaught of competition from the likes of MCI, Sprint, Alltel, and hundreds of others. I observed the staff was very professional but didn't interact with customers much. It seemed that they were used to taking orders over the phone, so most were unprepared for the instantly competitive environment. In the morning, they would roll in, read the newspaper, chat with one another, and have coffee. During lunch, many played pinochle in the lunchroom. One woman was of the three-martini lunch set and often came back to the office tipsy.

The branch manager was pre-occupied with a dispute over a revenue sharing agreement with Pacific Bell, as well as our joint customer, the State of California. There was plenty of activity designing data networks, optimizing the state's network, solving billing issues, and network outages. In time, the calm would all be blown up by the realization that the new AT&T and it progeny

Pacific Bell did not know how to work together. The provision of private line services for data stopped. It was a disaster unforeseen by the planners, and both companies suffered enormously, as did our customers caught in the middle. I learned that free-flowing information is the lifeblood of business. We paralyzed many businesses and damaged their operations. It was unforgivable. The paralysis inside of AT&T was complete and total.

Prior to our knowledge of the size and scope of the provisioning disaster, Branch Manager Don Lloyd asked me to help with his Quota Review Board presentation. Known as QRB, this is essentially a negotiation about how much revenue the sales staff is willing to commit to bringing in. It was mostly a futile exercise as the numbers got crammed down from the top, but it was entertaining. Each sales team came in with their sales plan so there was at least a notion of bottom to top input. At its conclusion, sales objectives were assigned to each sales team. Some months later, the compensation plan arrived from HQ and then the sales teams found out what products and services management wanted them to sell. It was quite convoluted, but it did give the order takers something to work on, even if much of it was fantasy.

During the sales teams' presentations, they all stated there had been no competitive incursions into their accounts and that AT&T garnered 99% of the available revenues. I was incredulous at these assertions given the amount of coverage our competitors were getting in the press and how visible they were in advertising. I asked Mr. Lloyd if I could do a research project and visit ten randomly selected accounts to find out what the competitive profile was like. He agreed, and I began setting appointments sans the account teams. Unsurprisingly, we were getting clobbered. All ten accounts were using at least one competitor. Some were using more than one. These accounts did not recall being called on by AT&T recently. Some of these accounts reduced their AT&T usage to half of their total. I asked to look at their billings with competitors to see if AT&T could save them money by consolidating services. They all agreed. To say it was an eye-opener was an understatement.

After reporting my findings, I asked to have these accounts assigned to me, as no AT&T representative had called on them. I was given the accounts as my "module," and began making proposals. Not all were converted, but many were. The days of sitting back and taking orders were over for the AT&T sales staff. Or not. Culture is a difficult thing to change. AT&T, at this time and place, did not have a sales culture. Management knew it, and the conversion would soon take place. Could these life-long AT&T employees make the transition?

AT&T brought in a number of former IBM executives to help make the transition in both sales ability and executive-level selling. A sales university was created in Denver, dubbed, "Darth Vader U," as it was housed in a dark glass encased building. As we soon discovered, the name was appropriate for what went on inside the building as well. Attendees were required to wear business attire, and jackets were to remain on during the entire class. These were large classes comprised of hundreds of people. The schedule was all day lectures and exercises, including presentations, and generally there were nighttime assignments. It was brutal. While I never witnessed this, it was rumored failures were met with a public display where the sales rep was handed an airplane ticket in front 150 other students and told to leave. "Tell your manager that you failed." This [urban] legend was completed with the "mythical" employee being terminated. I know the stress got to one colleague who went sleep walking in the nude, awakened only by the "click" of his hotel room door closing behind him. They had our complete attention. It was too much, too soon.

AT&T valued tenure, and I worked with many employees with 30-plus years of service; my co-worker Joan retired with 39 years of service. After several months of anguish and torture of valued employees, the program was terminated. In my group, we adopted some of the techniques, including critiquing written proposals, simulating competitors offers, filming sales presentations, and dissecting performances. I thought these techniques served us well. While difficult, we all improved our skills and success rate.

As competition took its toll, our employee count went down significantly. This process was heartless. The news came down about reductions in November. All employees were ranked on a bell curve, most of that was numerically based on sales results. The bottom ten percent were told around Thanksgiving that they would be "off Payroll effective 1/1," meaning by year's end. Happy Holidays!

As this was transpiring, I went through the certification process (it was so consuming and stressful I managed to close the garage door on my new car, damaging the roof). The certification program was a process to become a full-fledged account executive then later, account executive industry consultant. This was a promotion to "2nd level," and essentially provided tenure.

We were required to provide written documentation about a group of sales we consummated. The documentation of the each sale was used to judge our professionalism. Further, it was used to demonstrate our knowledge of the customer's business and processes, and to persuade clients to change the way their company did business by using services from AT&T. Failure to graduate to the next level in certain timeframes led to dismissal. It was a serious process. A board of branch managers and vice-presidents who reviewed your written submission convened to hear your oral presentation to determine your fate. You were provided with three submissions to progress. If unsuccessful you were terminated.

It was also an exercise in creative writing. It was absurd to believe that our account executives knew enough to recommend changes in the business operations of our customers. We did not deal with senior management at client companies. The typical interaction was with a telecom manager, who usually reported to the IT manager housed in the CFO organization. I think the commitment to this process was a vestige of the desire to compete with IBM whose products were more strategic to a business and thus led to more senior management interaction.

Over time, I was assigned the State of California as my account. They were the largest account in the branch. The division of revenues issue with Pacific Bell had been settled, and the State of California's Telecommunications Division wanted to upgrade its network. They acted as the provider (gatekeeper) of services to all of the state agencies, except the State Legislature. The state hired some consultants to develop the bid specifications and technical parameters. We had a long relationship with the staff; many of them did not like AT&T. The bid development and award process took some two years. Essentially, the state wanted to be a telephone company and own everything. Some of their requirements were superfluous. I recall going to a lunch at Frank Fat's, where politicians and lobbyists were known to convene. We dined with a senior state official where we attempted to dissuade them from this endeavor, citing the risk of obsolescence and cost. He laughed and said, "If we make a mistake, it's only $100 million." Welcome to big government.

We met with the consultants under the crazy notion that we could influence the bid specifications to our favor. Some ideas were accepted. However, the state's staff had a number of ideas that required us to bid items AT&T sold only to telephone companies, and certainly not through a junior sales team. The project was called CalNet and was the most arduous process I had gone through.

There were four separate submissions: Conceptual, Detailed Technical, Contract Terms, and Final with Pricing. We had to convince AT&T to let us bid certain items. I learned about technology and how systems work. I was privileged to work with members of Bell Labs, AT&T Network Systems, Operations, Provisioning, Power Systems, Boeing Computer Services, Tandem Computers, and TTSI software. The team slept on the couches in Bell Labs' Red Hill Facility and the basement of 795 Folsom Street in San Francisco as we stayed up for days writing the final bid response, some 20 volumes. When we finally finished at 2 a.m., we loaded the sets to be delivered in my boss' car (Richard M. Burk: best boss ever) and proceeded across the San Francisco Bay Bridge back to Sacramento. As luck would have it, the timing belt in his Subaru failed in the middle of the second span. Fortunately, a tow truck from CalTrans gave us a shove to the end of the bridge. Somehow, we were able to get the thing repaired in time to return to the office and submit our bid. We hired consultants to simulate the bids of our competitors; we were priced higher than GTE, and much higher than EDS. When asked of AT&T senior management why our authorized price was so high in comparison, his response was: "Kentucky Windage," which meant: to account for the wind while shooting a rifle at a distant target.

In state bid processes, the bids are revealed at the appointed time. The sealed boxes are opened and the volume containing the pricing is located. The one or two page price summary is read aloud and written on a white board. Two years of work came down to this. We got creamed. The consultants who prepared the pricing simulation had it exactly right. EDS was the low bid, next came GTE and then AT&T.

I walked out with Rich and began to cry.

We decided to protest the award. This was the only decision Rich Burk made that I thought was wrong after getting hundreds right. EDS was disqualified for non-compliance. There was an award proceeding where I gave the lead testimony as to why GTE was also non-compliant, and we should be granted the award. I recall Alan Tolman, the State of California's telecom director, laughing out loud.

After we lost, Rich Burk was promoted out and, in a crazy twist, I got promoted to take over his role in Sacramento. I now had sales responsibility for the entire state, including its universities as well as businesses in Northern California and Nevada. Although I was a loser, I was a winner! What a great company!

I had a great group. We continued to improve our skills and be successful in daunting market conditions. AT&T introduced new, competitive products and we won 16 accounts over with not a single loss. It took time, but the survivors at AT&T became very customer focused and learned to appreciate how important communications services are for any customer's business success. (We even won over E&J Gallo Winery, the most savvy and competent buyer on the planet.)

Having the State of California as a customer also gave me a different perspective from my internship on how hard many of them worked. The state employees were smart, dedicated, and had high expectations of us. At Health and Welfare, Dick Forsch,

Dale Goldsberry, and Glen Snow were my principle contacts, and we became friends. At General Services, Jerry Kilaney did not like AT&T much and was a bit of a pill, but we maintained a professional relationship even though our market share contracted significantly. There were many others whom I respected greatly. I was professionally enriched by the experience.

One of my customers, second in revenue only to the state, was a computer services firm who provided billing and other services to the cable industry. The firm was called Cable Data. Like most other companies, they had awarded some of their business to our competitors. Our provisioning crisis affected them dramatically as they relied on our data services to deliver their services. I began with them as their account executive. I was on site constantly with them: keeping them informed of the status of their orders; bringing specialists out to deal with transmission problems; bringing in other specialists to optimize their network design, and still others to help them make sense of our bills. It was a successful relationship but was severely tested when they opened a new data center in Braintree, Massachusetts. I asked what the back-up plan was if something went awry, as AT&T was constructing new facilities in the area to serve them. The response from Telecom Manager Dan Pringle was: "We've burned the bridge and there is no going back." Miraculously, we performed.

One of the senior management team members liked what we had done on the account. While I didn't meet with her much, I must have made a positive impression. When Maggie Wilderotter left Cable Data to join McCaw Cellular, she asked me to join her team.

THREE
enter the wireless revolution

WHEN I ACCEPTED THE OFFER, my father was apoplectic. He could not understand why I would leave a great company like AT&T, with the stability it provided, for an unknown company that offered a product he didn't think much of. (A generational shift, I suppose.)

The cellular business was in its infancy. The McCaw Cellular business operated under the brand Cellular One. I was hired as district director of sales and marketing.

I need to harken back to AT&T here for a bit. As part of the divestiture of the Bell companies, AT&T agreed to *give* them the cellular business along with the Yellow Pages. A business forecasting group in Bell Labs determined the cellular business was of little value in that less than one million customers would use the service by the turn of the twentieth century. They slightly missed by 30 million or so customers. Indeed, wireless communications are the most valuable asset in the telecom industry and may soon supplant wireline telecom for everything, including broadband internet service.

Each of the Bell companies was *given* a license and spectrum by the FCC. Two licenses were granted in a market: one for the Bell Companies (the B side) and one auctioned off by market area. The A side licenses were purchased by a diverse variety of groups for some $10 to $35 per person who lived in the market area. Many of these groups were speculative investors. Before this, Craig McCaw was running the family cable TV operations from his dorm room at Stanford. He sold the cable operation to Jack Kent Cooke. Mr. McCaw then used the proceeds to begin acquiring cellular markets around California, including Sacramento, Stockton and Modesto. His strategy was to emulate cable operators and acquire geographic clusters of markets. This was a brilliant strategy and provided strategic advantages over the seven Bell companies limited to a regional footprint. Additionally, Mr. McCaw used high-yield debt securities (junk bonds) to further fund network deployment and acquisitions.

One of the brilliant minds of finance, Michael Milken, midwifed this structure to enable the development of this new wireless industry. Mr. Milken later served time in prison for securities fraud. He has since been involved in a number of philanthropic endeavors and is an upstanding citizen as well as a cancer survivor.

When I began at Cellular One, the operation had graduated from reselling service on PacTel's network to operating our own assets. There were no sales channels save for selling through dealers and agents. The company paid large commissions, in some cases to a rag-tag group of individuals. Large consumer retail (such as the now defunct Circuit City and the Good Guys) was in its infancy as a sales channel. I was responsible for an internal sales force. It was a bit like the Wild West… chaotic. This was particularly so after being in the regimented sales organization at AT&T.

Qwest for Truth ...and Change

During my first week on the job, one of the founding management members, Jon Chapple, paid me a visit. He sat on the corner of my desk (that made quite an impression after the regal management at AT&T) and told me I needed to develop a simple compensation plan for the sales force. I began to describe my plan architecture, when he interrupted me and said, "That's too complicated. Try to get it on a single sheet of paper." I had just come from AT&T where the compensation plan was a five-inch thick, three-ring binder. What a contrast!

Our task was to build a professional sales force that served business rather than anyone wanting a phone. It took some time to put a saddle on these wild mustangs, but in time their proposals and presentations made us all proud. They resisted the coat and necktie evolution at first, but later began to appreciate it. I also had the opportunity to build out a company-owned retail strategy. I relied on many others to bring this about this pioneering effort in the company. We turned out to be quite successful in serving customers, as well as lowering customer acquisition costs dramatically. I believe that this company-owned retail channel became the most productive, efficient, and important part of the industry's distribution system (save for the online component that came later).

The marketing aspect to the role was new to me. There were a large number of people inside the company, and in our advertising and public relations agencies, who were instrumental to our success. Kind of. The real success was the product itself, where people immediately understood the benefits of mobile communications. They literally beat a path to our door to get their phone. We didn't need to be that clever—and we weren't. We did differentiate ourselves from the Bell operators because of the strategy Mr. McCaw envisioned: national coverage. We were the only operator that developed a national network, which made a huge difference to high-value customers who traveled extensively, and to our corporate accounts.

In this role, I got my first introduction to product development. This entailed developing rate plans for specific customer segments. The company had a program I attended called Revenue U (for University) in Salt Lake City. The design of the rate plans was based on the 7-11 Slurpee. You read that right. You could get a little rate plan with just a few minutes included, or, you could get the next size up with many more minutes included, or, go for the Big Gulp and get tons of minutes for an incrementally small upcharge. If the customer did not use all of the minutes, they were still thought to be generally satisfied. Obviously, this was prior to rollover and when customers bought a phone service, rather than data service as we do today where the voice minutes are a throw away. This was also my first trip in a private jet, (how cool).

We were mostly marketing the product on the basis of price with additional promotions to reduce sign up fees. In those days, we began by selling the phone undiscounted. The first flip phones with a cradle and antenna installed in a vehicle ran $3,500. Later, at the behest of Mrs. Wilderotter (Maggie), we began subsidizing phones. The sizable commissions we were paying dealers and retailers enabled this. As phone prices fell, dealers were able to offset the subsidy with a fat commission payment. With the cost of smartphones today, carriers have moved away from this model.

In 1995, Mrs. Wilderotter took a role at the corporate office in Kirkland, Washington. It wasn't long before I became interested in following her there. While I never reported directly to Maggie,

I felt she was my sponsor and mentor. I went to visit her and see what opportunities might be available.

As a precursor, the company was organized into regions. The regions were fiercely independent and ran their own marketing campaigns (some of which were so awful they were inducted into the Hall of Shame). This regional plan meant that the headquarters staff was quite small. The regions also had control over their rate plans and that had morphed into some 2,300 versions. There were not compelling reasons to offer that number of "Slurpee choices." We outsourced our billing, and this complexity was getting expensive.

I took my family up to Seattle to visit and see what opportunities were available, look at real estate, visit the office, and the like. As it turns out, that weekend was a snowy one. Our families got together at Maggie's house to say farewell. They lived in a hilly area called Woodinville and my rear wheel rental car could not make it up the hill. Maggie had an idea…we would have her husband, Jay, give us a shove up the hill in his pick-up truck. Maggie, not wanting to damage either vehicle, grabbed an outdoor furniture cushion and placed it between the two vehicles as we began this futile effort. As I look at this senior executive holding a cushion between two traction-less vehicles in a snowstorm, I thought, *many things could go wrong here, not least my career.* The truck pushing the rental car did not work. I decided to turn around and see if I could get enough momentum from afar to make it up the hill and get out of Dodge. I recall rolling down the window and shouting, "Bonzai!" as I raced past Maggie, fearing my career had ended much the same as a Kamikaze pilot's.

I did accept a position in Kirkland in Product Development. This was a wonderful opportunity and I learned a great deal and participated in several significant developments. Most importantly, I worked with the group that launched the first text messaging service (known as short messaging service or SMS). Stew Chapin led this effort. We really had no idea what the use of this feature would be, but thought it could be useful in business. As opposed to the Bell Labs guys who missed cellular, this product exceeded all forecasts. It is my understanding the person who came up with the idea did not patent it. Oh well, they likely missed out on billions of dollars in royalties. The design of the system was brilliant and took its cue from alphanumeric pagers, but was even better as it used space in the control channel, thus not impacting voice transmission capacity. (As an aside, the innovation of Twitter is analogous as it was premised on the auto-reply "out-of-office" message used by many e-mail systems. Very clever.)

I also had the opportunity to work on the development of Digital One Rate, which is the product plan that bundled local calling, long distance, messaging, and voice mail in a single offering. This product ushered in the era of cannibalizing the home telephone. During my time in Kirkland, AT&T acquired the company. It seemed their strategy was to combine a cellular offer with home phone service in an attempt to save the consumer long distance business. There was even an AT&T business unit that sold AT&T long distance service to cellular users. I recall a meeting in New Jersey, AT&T's headquarters at the time, where I had to tell this division manager that our Digital One Rate plan was going to end his $130 million business. I told him it was inevitable and it was part of why AT&T paid $11.5 billion to acquire us. He did not like me much.

The merger between AT&T and McCaw was made more complicated as the cultures of the companies differed greatly. Additionally, being part of AT&T required a bit more discipline that ran counter to the various regions, which operated in a fiercely independent manner. One of the initiatives that came out of this was that Maggie agreed to consolidate our 2,300 rate plans to 100 with our contract biller. I was the bearer of this news. Simultaneously, the interactions with AT&T's consumer unit became testy as their business was under intense pressure. It was a $20 billion business and was rapidly losing market share. It seemed that each week I was flying between Seattle and New Jersey. I recall a meeting where we were discussing the possibility of integrating our bill inside the AT&T long distance bill. We were dissecting AT&T's billing process. There must have been 50 people in the room and not one of them could describe the end-to-end process of how a bill was generated. One person would describe their element, pass it on, then the next, then the next, and so on. I left wondering how they ever got a bill out the door.

I had many rewarding experiences at McCaw/AT&T Wireless Services. I worked with great people and was part of a terrific corporate culture. Maggie departed the company for a start up in San Francisco: Wink Communications.

I decided that I was not that fond of Seattle. Living on an airplane is awful. Working with AT&T again was impossible. The wireless business and the residential long distance business were diametrically opposed, and wireless was going to win, but AT&T owned us and had a numerical advantage. My career was stymied.

Then one day, I received a call from a former AT&T colleague who I'd met during the State of California CalNet project. Steve Jacobsen called and told me he had left AT&T and joined forces with Joe Nacchio in Denver at a new start up called Qwest. He asked me if I would like to come to Denver and check it out. (Manna from Heaven.)

Steve was an operations manager in Oakland and was driven. His father was a senior executive at AT&T with a long career. A long time ago he and I both interviewed for the job as Joe Nacchio's executive assistant. Steve got the role. I was told my educational background was lacking. It worked out great. Steve had the opportunity to attend the Sloan program at MIT where he developed a relationship with Joe Nacchio, which led him to a senior role at Qwest.

This was an easy thing to say yes to when he offered me the job. I accepted on June 23, 1997, the day Qwest became a public company trading on the NASDAQ under the ticker QWST.

As Director of Consumer Long Distance, I was to develop the consumer long distance business and its sales channels. It was odd from a couple of perspectives.

At the time, Qwest was a construction company that was going to be an underlying provider to other telecom companies (a carrier's carrier or wholesaler). Qwest was supposed to be a fiber optics based new-age company. So why sell commodity long distance in a shrinking market? Perhaps it was a bit of Joe Nacchio's revenge. He headed AT&T's consumer unit and was passed over to succeed CEO Robert E. Allen at AT&T. Even worse, he was passed over by an outsider, John Walter from RR Donnelly. AT&T historically promoted from within (historically from the ranks of Illinois Bell). Mr. Walter resigned under board pressure nine months after taking the job. Perhaps Joe Nacchio wanted to build a retail business with a brand and higher stock market valuations rather than be a wholesaler.

Qwest was very much a start-up when I arrived. There were a couple of consultants running the IT department. In this business your IT and billing capability determine what products you can offer as well at the quality of your customer interaction. It was less than world class. There were no distribution channels, so we started with multi-level marketing groups. Others in the industry had done so successfully. Yikes!

There was an offering at the time that allowed a customer to dial a five-digit access code to bypass (or "dial around") their long distance provider, and use your network (Qwest's was 10056). It was a bit like cheating on your provider behind their back.

The Qwest voice network was pretty lightweight then. We identified target markets where we had capacity and mailed out our offer. We blew the network up. We quickly learned we had very little capacity to get customers to the network and rendered more busy signals than calls. Fortunately, we did not tarnish the Qwest brand as the marketing name was QNC. Later, as we matured and added capacity, we began telemarketing to acquire customers. We hired third parties to make calls on our behalf—and it could be fairly described as a zoo. The individuals interrupting your dinner hour were referred to as: "Purple Mohawks," which described their appearance. I am reminded of a Mark Twain quote: "It is my heart-warm and world-embracing Christmas hope and aspiration that all of us—the high, the low, the rich, the poor, the admired, the despised, the loved, the hated, the civilized, the savage—may eventually be gathered together in a heaven of everlasting rest and peace and bliss—except for the inventor of the telephone." (From a December 23, 1890 a letter to the editor of the *New York World* newspaper.)

We developed an advertising campaign around a character named "Bob" who worked for a long distance company. The premise was that everyone hated their long distance provider. (Perhaps it was the dinnertime sales calls from the purple Mohawks?) We were supposed to be a brash upstart company, but this campaign was apparently too much. "Bob" was shown on the ledge of a tall building filled with suicidal thoughts; when the people below discovered he worked for the hated long-distance company, they encouraged him to jump. In another version "Bob" was in a hospital bed being visited by an Irish priest, who upon hearing he worked for a long distance company, began choking him. There was quite a backlash when the essence of the campaign was leaked. Suicide prevention groups were furious. Joe Nacchio was furious. Steve and I were elated our services were not terminated. The ad campaign was.

I did manage to get promoted and worked on several important deals. During this timeframe, the Bell companies were itching to get into the long distance business, but were precluded from doing so under the terms of the divestiture accord. There emerged a novel legal theory that the Bell companies could "team" with long distance companies acting as a sales agent and a billing and customer care agent under arms-length agreements. I spearheaded these efforts with Ameritech and US West. These companies would sign up customers and send us data files that contained the information required to convert the customer to Qwest long distance. The weakness of our IT systems was exposed under this avalanche of new business. Days, nights, and weekends were consumed by trying to process these orders. Disaster. In some respects it was fortunate the regulators put an end to the practice of teaming.

Qwest for Truth ...and Change

Later, I had the opportunity to work on the most consequential deal in my career. The teaming relationship between Qwest and the Bell companies took a different tack by looking at how business customers could benefit by receiving services from two companies designed to appear as one. The regulatory environment was evolving, as well. This opportunity was explored in depth with both BellSouth and Southwestern Bell. Southwestern Bell wanted something different: an agreement for Qwest to provide to them a litany of services under a guaranteed declining cost structure, underpinned by the belief costs will continue to decline in telecom services due to the advent of fiber-optics. They would commit to a revenue guarantee over the term of the agreement, lasting several years. We flew to San Antonio on the company jet to meet with their senior team. My future boss, Lewis O. Wilks, did all the talking. All of it. It was akin to a three-hour filibuster. Surprisingly, they agreed to another meeting.

This time the meeting was in Colorado at the Hemmingway Lodge (so named as Earnest Hemmingway stayed there some months prior to his demise). It was owned by Qwest founder Philip Anschutz. It was a hunting lodge with a nine-hole golf course, fishing stream, skeet range, and a huge log structure filled with art, taxidermy specimens, and Western artifacts. After playing golf and partaking in some of the other activities offered, we had dinner around an enormous table. Then, we gathered in separate groups to discuss prospects. For some reason, Mr. Nacchio had taken up smoking cigars. A number of us indulged in these fine cigars from Mr. Anschutz's humidor (none had labels). We were outside by the stream where I laid it out: These guys were not a good match for us because, among other things, their price concession demand principle.

Next stop was BellSouth. The BellSouth employees we worked with were terrific people. They were knowledgeable, dedicated, smart, patient, articulate, and generally easy to get along with. Mike Doscher and Bill Ficklin were the key players at my level. Very calm and thoughtful, they spoke with a slight Southern drawl and always based their positions on, "What do you believe in," referring to the migration of services to the world of the Internet Protocol. There was no sense of hostility as with Southwestern Bell. Part of the issue with Southwestern Bell was my counterpart had a real chip on his shoulder. I'm not sure if it was because he just didn't like the prospect of a tie-up with Qwest, or was it some deep seeded animosity rooted in the fact his brother is the famous actor Jack Wagner and he was toiling in the telecom industry. He was a good golfer—not as good as his famous brother, though.

The BellSouth people had no such baggage. It did not take long for us to build the outline of what the relationship would consist of and what each party would bring to the effort. Clearly, they had longstanding ties to many large customers and could enable Qwest sales teams access to decision makers. Earlier, Qwest had acquired LCI, and we (thankfully) transitioned to their IT infrastructure. LCI's entire systems architecture was developed by them (Rick Sunderman, in particular) and they wrote all of its software code. Our relationship commenced in 1999 just prior to the concern in the industry about the effect of Y2K in IT systems. As the systems were written internally, it was imperative to have the code documented and tested to insure its operability as 1999 turned into 2000. It all worked fine, leading some to believe the whole Y2K thing was a conspiracy designed to drive consulting contracts.

The essence of the teaming relationship was to piggyback Qwest sales teams with Bellsouth's, and each would sell its respective services.

Qwest for Truth ...and Change

A single point of contact would be established for installation, repair, and billing support and a joint operations center would manage these functions using Qwest's IT systems. Qwest's position was to make only traditional telecom services available. Thus, the crown jewels of Qwest, its Internet portfolio, were off limits. I ran point on this hocus-pocus until very late in the process.

We were holed up for two weeks in the Citicorp Tower in New York City writing the agreements and negotiating. BellSouth was incredulous that we were attempting to withhold access to the services that were the whole point of the deal. One evening, Joe Nacchio strolled in wearing a baby blue cashmere sweater and caved into every demand they had. I looked like a complete idiot. *There must have been more at play here*, I thought.

Concomitant with our agreement was a commitment on BellSouth's part to ensure Qwest received $500 million in services revenue. Once BellSouth received government permission to sell the services, Qwest would vacate the market in the BellSouth region. This was the largest commercial deal I ever worked on. The bigger deal was the agreement by BellSouth to acquire a 9.9% stake in Qwest. This stake was worth $3.5 billion and BellSouth required a portion to come from Mr. Anschutz's personal holdings. Mr. Anschutz's stake was worth $1.57 billion, cash.

The relationship was consummated in April of 1999, and implementation began. There were difficulties in operations, but nothing catastrophic. The Y2K concerns never materialized. It seemed both sides were committed to the relationship.

The relationship materially changed only a couple of months later when Qwest and US West announced a merger. There were plenty of questions about how this might affect the relationship.

Qwest would be required to divest its services in the 14 states served by US West, thus blowing a hole in the notion of a national service offering. Importantly, BellSouth was concerned that Qwest management may lose interest and focus while dealing with a merger.

Periodic meetings were held at senior management levels to discuss progress and deal with any significant issues. I recall being in one of these meetings where BellSouth security came in and swept the room for bugs (listening devices) when our senior executives were called out of the meeting and left the premises. *What was going on?* I felt that we were disrespectful at best. It was days later that I caught wind of what transpired. The team jetted to Bonn, Germany to hold merger discussions with Deutche Telecom. It was supposed to be top secret, but these things get around. I was eventually told that Ron Sommer, their chief executive, was "wetting his pants" over the prospect of acquiring Qwest. I understood the discussed valuation for Qwest was stratospheric.

This created a litany of issues given the pending merger with US West, as well as the relationship with BellSouth. It was understood the regulatory review of a foreign entity, that was majority owned by the German government, would be lengthy and contentious. A notion was advanced for the Qwest/US West merger to be tabled and allow Deutche Telecom to acquire Qwest and subsequently work out the regulatory issues of all three companies being combined. I was told US West wanted no part of that deal. The story at Qwest was that US West was struggling to make its numbers and did not want to wait that long. There was discussion about terminating the merger with US West and proceeding with Deutche Telecom. US West took the story public, indicating Qwest would face litigation of a similar sort to the Pennzoil case. In that case,

Qwest for Truth ...and Change

Texaco interfered with a merger between Getty Oil and Pennzoil. Pennzoil sued, prevailed, and won an award of $11.5 billion. It eventually settled out for less, but it was a big deal at the time. Qwest wanted no part of that and moved to consummate the merger with US West.

An interesting element of the Anschutz Companies' ownership was a provision in the Employee Stock Option Plan. Stock options represent a form of compensation, increasing in value as the firm's share price rises and they mature over time: typically, a four-year period. When exercised, the recipient receives the difference in the original price at the issue date and the current stock price. Stock options generally represent the largest creation of wealth for employees in corporate America. Anschutz'/Qwest stock option plan provided that if the Anschutz entities ownership stake fell below 20% it had the same effect as a "Change of Control" provision where all shares vested immediately (no waiting). All stock options issued to certain employees under this accord vested upon the closing of the merger. The provision was applied only to employees granted options early in Qwest's lifecycle as it was later modified. This was a big deal. This provision will be dealt with later in the Qwest culture section.

Prior to the closing of the merger of Qwest and US West, significant discussions were held with BellSouth about acquiring the 90% of Qwest it didn't own, and perhaps acquiring both Qwest and US West. Due diligence was performed and both sides poured over documents, presentations, and spreadsheets. I recall BellSouth relied heavily on a single consultant to help them sort through a portion of the operational synergies. I distinctly remember him as he often wore a bright yellow linen shirt with white linen pants, and slip on shoes with no socks. BellSouth was a pretty staid company and this seemed out of character. The consultant was also quite caustic. It was clear from the outset he was not going to support a larger combination. The Qwest senior team members were pissed. They believed BellSouth had no balls and were too timid to be a great partner in the rough and tumble world of telecom, let alone in the emerging world of IP-based services. Qwest was comprised of the emperors of the new universe; Bellsouth were knuckle draggers. Qwest management did indeed focus on the US West merger and the fact they would all vest and be wealthy. The relationship we worked so hard to build became contentious and unhealthy.

As this was happening, I had been promoted and moved on to product management. I became the ninth product management leader in the last twenty-four months. While Joe Nacchio appreciated my work in the BellSouth transaction (for which I received no additional compensation), he was reluctant to have me lead the effort for the crucial development and maturation of the IP product portfolio. It happened quickly as product management leader #8 melted down after only a couple of weeks in the role. Other supporters on the management team convinced Mr. Nacchio to accept me in this role. This was an awesome opportunity as there were very talented people on the team as product managers, marketing managers, and people who understood the dynamics of the emerging revolution in IP services. They were zealots. We were changing the world. It was good. No, it was great.

I quickly discovered that the unit needed consistency and stability. The hard part about these products is the process: you have to have all of the functional areas of the business involved. Thus, it requires building coalitions with: engineering, operations, IT, billing, marketing, sales, customer care, etc. It requires competence in knowing how the process works, as well as extreme attention to detail. We focused on these areas and were very successful. We grew revenues to over a billion dollars in two years. We had some industry firsts also that included the initial commercial launch of Voice over the Internet (VoIP) and the first commercial Virtual Private Network (VPN).

Products were introduced at a rapid rate in a changing environment. We were spending mountains of capital on building new things such as Internet data centers called CyberCenters, hosted exchange service, content distribution networks, IP back-bones, hubs, peering arrangements, and access networks. It seemed we couldn't invest enough in all of the opportunities appearing on the horizon. There was a novel idea circulating about different ways to build new product platforms. It used a unique business model and changed the financial characteristics of how new product introductions performed. It was a way to build new platforms, not consume capital, and actually generate revenue to offset the loss of EBITDA typically associated with product launches. As I came into the role, one or two of these novel transactions were in process.

FOUR

*certain transactions...and cobras
...be wary of their bite*

A NEW PRODUCT DEVELOPMENT breakthrough that enables the introduction of new products without consuming capital and generates immediate profits may sound too good to be true. At Qwest, certain transactions had these characteristics. One variety was referred to as COBRA. This product development strategy was the brainchild of David Boast who joined Qwest from competitor, UUNET. COBRA is actually an acronym that stands for Central Office Basic Rate Access.

Not so long ago, the Internet was accessed by using a modem and a telephone line to place a call to a distant modem, granting access to the datacenter hosting the content you sought. An end-user would subscribe to the service, paying a monthly fee to use the Internet. The Internet service providers (ISP) at the time were the likes of America on Line (AOL), EarthLink, CompuServe and many, many others. AOL relied on companies like UUNET to build large banks of modems in many different geographical locations so their customers could make a local (free) call to the Internet. This allowed AOL to focus on developing its content, user interface, mail services, and the marketing of its services on a large scale. The marketing generally consisted of mailing a disk to the user. They were to insert the disk into their computer; the disk contained the browser and instructions on how to connect to the network, as well as billing information. When the user wanted to access the Internet, this software established the connection, unlike the "always on" connections we are familiar with now.

There were many new market entrants to cover the geography. The changing regulatory environment, specifically the Telecom Act of 1996, enabled a class of companies called CLEC's, or Competitive Local Exchange Carriers. The companies were alternatives to the Bell companies. The Bell companies offered similar capabilities, where they would house the modems in their telephone facilities and enable interconnection to the ISP. The Bell companies had a structural limitation in that they could not carry traffic outside of their local area. The new market entrants (CLEC's) did not have these same limitations. As is typically the case, the new market entrants had better ideas about the service, did not have an existing revenue stream to protect, and were much more nimble. We see examples of this constantly as new entrants disrupt existing markets, for example, Amazon decimating retailers, Facebook altering advertising, and Google (Alphabet) micro-targeting customers through data mining rather than mass advertising.

My introduction to a COBRA transaction was with a CLEC in Denver (ICG Communications). The idea was Qwest could use its purchasing power and buy the modems at a steep discount and resell them to the CLEC at a profit. The equipment would be housed in the CLEC's building. Qwest would also build interconnection capabilities for the CLEC using its network facilities. As well, Qwest would enter into an agreement to lease some of the modem capacity for its own use and resell it to its customers. The beauty of COBRA was we could generate instant profit from the equipment sale, without the risk of obsolescence or ownership, and still use the service to generate additional revenues from our customers. Thus, Qwest was using others' money in lieu of investing its own capital. Below are two graphs depicting a traditional product "S" curve, and the COBRA-style "S" curve.

Typically, the introduction of a product (any product) entails an investment in development, marketing, and training, among many other elements. As the product gains market share, it grows up the "S" curve. In its later stages (called harvest) the product is very profitable, but revenues are slowing. The "S" depicts its revenue trajectory. Typically, product managers want to have a number of products in various stages along the path of the curve. As the COBRA model shows, the introduction of the product is such that it is never below the break-even point (BEP).

COBRA Revenue Effect on revenue and EBITDA versus traditional product launches

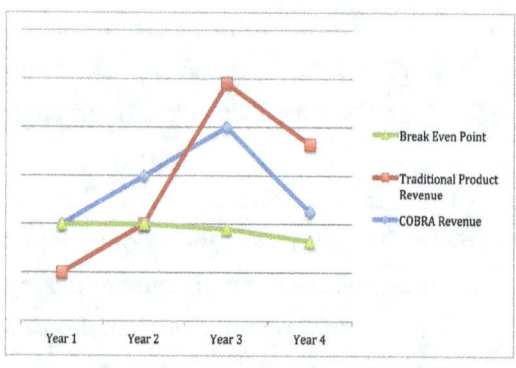

Traditional product launches consume EBITDA as expenses are incurred prior to the product generating revenue. In the case of COBRA, the sale of equipment generates a profit thereby consuming no EBITDA prior to the generation of revenues, at least theoretically.

Qwest for Truth ...and Change

I didn't focus too much on this initial transaction with ICG, as there were plenty of other issues to attend to. A consultant was managing the project. Since some of my team members expressed confidence in her and the project's success, I was not spending time on it.

Suddenly, there was consideration for a number of these projects. We had aspirations for competing with AOL nationally and developing content and other services for our customers. We were also developing a strategic relationship with Microsoft and wanted to carry their MSN traffic. This ISP business was booming as AOL and the others were acquiring millions of new customers.

At Qwest in 1999, on St. Patrick's Day, there was a senior management meeting where the product team presented its plans for the Multiple Services Internet Platform (MSIP). This was a plan to build out a nationwide network that would enable an array of Internet based services, including dial-up Internet access. I was not present for this meeting as it preceded my becoming the product management leader. The meeting was legendary in that the product management leader at the time, Nayel Shaffei, became animated, and began running around the board room table while shouting, "You're a dinosaur, you're a dinosaur," expressing that the company was moving too slowly and thinking too narrowly. It was from this meeting that approval was granted to pursue the build out of a national network to provide 95% of the U.S. population access to the Internet.

While the plan was approved, the ability to actually do it was less clear. There was always a constant battle for capital at Qwest. I recall the company was spending 7, 8, and $9billion of capital in consecutive years, yet there never seemed to be enough to feed our ambitions.

The COBRA structure seemed ideal to fill the void. I was introduced to a CLEC named KMC Telecom (by our consultant, Sue Carver) who was going to be our partner in one of these transactions. I became intimately involved in the negotiations and the drafting of the agreements. We used outside counsel and had individuals from finance and operations participating in the negotiations. Accounting guidance was provided to our finance participants directly from Arthur Andersen.

It was made crystal clear to me the transaction had to have certain elements to suit our financial objectives and meet the legal and accounting requirements. First, the equipment purchase agreement had to make clear that Qwest was selling the modems to KMC (in this case) and that they had to take physical possession of the equipment, accept the risk of loss, and accept title. This enabled recognition of the revenue accruing from the sale. Our financial team intended to recognize the entirety of the revenue immediately; this was paramount to maintaining the shape of the S curve. A second agreement was entered into detailing the terms under which Qwest would lease services back from KMC. These two agreements had to be completely separate with no reference to the other. No terms could crossover between agreements. The agreements were executed simultaneously. While not technically accurate from an accounting perspective (I was informed) the transactions resembled a "sale and leaseback."

Several agreements followed in the race to rapidly build out the network. Internal arguments took place within Qwest as the Operations Department was concerned about KMC's ability to manage a national project. Others were concerned and contended that we should be building these networks internally, using our people and capital, because that is what telecoms traditionally do. They argued that we could deliver a better service, more reliably.

The follow-on agreements were very large, worth hundreds of millions of dollars. We reached the point where we had enough capacity to serve the country and now we needed to get busy filling the capacity we purchased from KMC. There was another element of the COBRA agreements that required us to commit to paying for a certain amount of capacity, whether or not we needed or used it. This enabled KMC to get the financing necessary to complete the purchase. The provision was known as "Hell or High Water:" Qwest pays come hell or high water. The snake bites back.

The other deadly element of these COBRA transactions is one can get addicted to the rush of revenues. The pain of the transaction comes down the road and only if you don't use the contracted capacity. If the forecast for revenue comes in a little light it might be tempting to make the COBRA dance. These deals can be "papered up" quickly. Equipment can be manufactured and shipped in a 30-day window. KMC was more than willing to build more capacity assuming the "Hell or High Water" provision was included.

I recall having this conversation with my boss, Lewis O. Wilks, although he denies it in his deposition. (He also denied being my boss, that we were peers, laughably suggesting that I was free to do whatever deals I wanted to do.) He directed me to accelerate and increase the size of a COBRA transaction as part of the "Initiatives" process at Qwest where revenue gaps had been identified, and the initiatives were actions used to close those gaps. As part of the initiatives process later in the year, Mr. Wilks asked me if we could do another COBRA transaction. I told him we had enough capacity for our forecasts; my answer was no. He told me that we needed a deal on the order of $65 million and I needed to figure it out. (I indicated the number was $80 million in my deposition). We did another deal.

In time, even more initiatives were requested of me. I convened my team and asked, "What are areas where we could bolster our capacity, improve service, or create a competitive advantage? What is on your wish list that we haven't asked for capital yet?" We developed a business case and architecture for an IP aggregation strategy. We did have a need in the product manager's plan for such a capability, but it was developed in response to an "initiative," rather than being a component of our current plan.

This sort of activity became the reason for the fall of the house of Qwest. In another area of the business, similar activities were taking place. These activities were the sale of dark fiber, lit fiber, and wavelengths under an arrangement known as an Indefeasible Right to Use or IRU. Typically, an IRU grants the customer use of the facilities for a term of 20 years. Very large dollar amounts were involved. During the waning days of Mr. Nacchio's tenure, these IRU transactions took the form of "contemporaneous swaps." The most notorious of these were between Qwest and Global Crossing where the swap of portions of each other's networks were immediately recorded as revenue and contained large profit margins.

THE ACCOUNTING PRACTICES AT QWEST were never put on trial. There is an argument to be made that the IRU-based capacity swaps were used to fill coverage holes, supplement international routes, and create shorter rings to enhance survivability, and to provide physical route diversity, and were thus legitimate. The recording of revenues associated with such swaps is an area I have no expertise in. Another technical accounting issue identified by the SEC was the need to maintain a separate inventory of dark fiber, wavelengths, etc. from the inventory used internally. This would have consumed even more capital.

With respect to the COBRA transactions, an argument was that the broadband revolution was imminent, dial-up was pedestrian (especially for a fiber optics-based revolutionary), and one should not invest precious capital in assets that will be useless forthwith. Qwest did acquire US West who was rapidly investing in broadband Internet (DSL) that was more consistent with the profile of Internet zealots. Some used this line of reasoning in their depositions to justify the transactions and their legitimacy, rather than the role they played in meeting revenue and EBITDA targets.

After the fall of the house of Qwest, new management restated most of these contracts to recognize the revenue ratably (i.e., over the term of the contract). This choice served to benefit the newly installed management team as they reported increasing revenue streams. It also appeared to satisfy the regulator's view of appropriate accounting for revenue recognition.

FIVE

genuity — the real deal; having genuine character
—Urban Dictionary

GENUITY WAS an Internet services company that was created due to the acquisition of GTE by Bell Atlantic to form what is now Verizon (note that many more mergers created what is now Verizon). Regulatory necessity required GTE to spin off its assets not related to local telephone service. One of the assets that GTE spun off was a national fiber optic network constructed by ... Qwest.

Genuity was created with the spin-off. In addition to the fiber optic network, the new company also included the burgeoning Internet operations GTE had assembled. GTE had acquired BBN and paired it with its Internet backbone to form GTE Internetworking. BBN was *the* pioneer in the Internet space and was involved in building some of the earliest networks, including ARPANET, which ultimately became the foundation for the current Internet architecture. Genuity operated with the designation AS 1, denoting its role in the founding of the Internet (AS- autonomous system; Qwest's AS was 209). The company was successful in marketing its services and became the primary transport network for AOL.

A number of events conspired for me to get to know Genuity. The merger of Qwest with US West resulted in my assuming selected product management responsibilities from both companies, exclusively in the Internet arena. (There was a separate product group responsible for traditional telecom services.) US West had a product for Internet service provider's known as Custom Remote Access Service or CRAS (Telecoms are notorious for acronyms). This was a product team that now reported to me. CRAS and COBRA are the same functionally, but CRAS was owned and operated by the carrier, while COBRA was a 'sale and leaseback' arrangement. Genuity was a customer of CRAS and had been in discussions with the US West sales team about a much bigger deployment.

On September 12, 2000, I was scheduled to speak at a conference in Boston. The following day, the 13th (Friday the 13th fell on a Wednesday that year), I was to meet our sales executive, Susan Ershler, for a meeting with Genuity at their headquarters in Burlington, Massachusetts. While I was nominally familiar with the proposal, it seemed I was present to show our love for them. Here they were, sending in an executive in a suit who showed interest. I was then senior vice-president of Qwest Internet Solutions, and was there to get this deal done. Apparently, the transaction had been under discussion for several months, but was stalled. I was briefed on the elements of the transaction and where disagreements existed.

The proposed transaction was odd, to say the least. I was told Genuity was not interested in owning any equipment. They wanted to have a structure with a large upfront payment; I was told Wall Street valued capital investments for Internet companies in those heady days. Wall Street was also looking for Genuity to show a declining cost structure for its monthly port fees it charged to AOL, thereby improving its operating margins. They were looking for an exclusivity arrangement where Qwest would not compete with them for AOL's business. The desire was to close the transaction by the end of the month. No problem.

We went into the meeting and made introductions and exchanged pleasantries. We began with a discussion about the elements of the transaction. I was not immersed in the details, but the elements quickly became clear to me. To meet the requirement that Genuity had for a large upfront payment, the proposal on the table was to modify an existing contract and charge an early termination fee where one had not previously existed. I thought, *holy crap, we could go to jail for this!* To me, this deal was never going to happen as proposed.

I got up and went to the white board and sketched out a couple elements of what a COBRA transaction looks like. I felt certain that it would meet their requirement to pay up front. (Naturally, Qwest sales expressed a desire to book $79.6 million by the end of the month.) The numbers could be worked to engineer the upfront cost, and the ongoing monthly cost, to suit the preferences of both sides. Genuity got over the issue of owning the equipment and agreed to accept title and risk of loss based on the following term: Qwest would maintain "custodial control" of the equipment Genuity purchased as it would operate in Qwest's physical locations.

To deal with the physical acceptance of the equipment, an arrangement was made where it would be shipped and reside in a Graybar facility under contract by Genuity. It would have to be air shipped to make the end of month deadline. These crucial elements were required to recognize the revenues by month's end. This follows the playbook engineered by Qwest finance with the guidance of Arthur Andersen.

I did not negotiate the terms of this contract. (Or, the two contracts I should say.) I was not actively involved in this deal as it was being negotiated. There are plenty of e-mails that circulated among the members of both the sales and finance teams as the terms and language of the agreements were finalized; my name rarely appears on them. I did authorize the equipment to be purchased from Lucent Technologies. I did authorize the equipment to be air shipped and delivered to the Graybar warehouse.

The Project Management organization was evaluated on a number of factors: We were incented to grow recurring service revenues across all products. My team would have been rewarded for a transaction structured like CRAS where we built a service and Genuity paid for it monthly. My group did not handle equipment sales, and we received no credit for the $100 million in equipment sold to Genuity in this transaction. Stated fairly, this transaction, as all COBRA deals, were to the *detriment* of my unit's results. I received no compensation for my limited involvement in this transaction. Ms. Ershler and her team were compensated as she stated in her deposition. (Some $300,000 paid in commissions; Ms. Ershler stated in her deposition she received $17,000).

Arthur Andersen rendered its opinion on the transaction in a memorandum dated November 3, 2000. "The above agreements are not contingent upon each other. Based on the discussion above, AA concludes that the equipment sale and service agreements are in compliance with SAB 101. As the four concerns for revenue recognition are met, and as AA determined the two agreements to be separate non-contingent agreements both priced at fair value, AA concludes accounting treatment to recognize revenue from equipment sale (sic) upfront to be appropriate."

It would appear both sides got what they wanted. It took some effort and certainly financial engineering, but it did not appear any documents were withheld nor any side agreements created to obfuscate the true construct and terms of this deal.

SIX
can i call you joe?

I ADOPTED Sarah Palin's approach to Joe Biden in the 2008 Vice-Presidential debate for the title of this chapter. She used it because she (reportedly) kept referring to him as "O'Biden" in the debate prep. I think it personalized then Senator Biden.

I use it here to personalize Joseph P. Nacchio, the Chief Executive Officer of Qwest. First let me share some background on Joe.

Joe seems like such a simple name for a man of great complexity. Joe is the son of Frank and Carmela Nacchio (pronounced na-shee-oh) and has two brothers, one older, one younger. Joe's father was a bartender. The family moved around a lot and I recall him saying once that he had lived in all five boroughs of New York City. Joe was reportedly a very good student and a member of the track team. Joe attended NYU and earned a degree in electrical engineering.

The urban legend is that Joe was to interview with P&G, but walked into the wrong room where AT&T was conducting interviews. (Serendipity?) He was offered a position and began his AT&T career as an engineer. Joe received several promotions, resulting from his tenacity and ability to get stuff done, as well as being very smart. While he is irascible and can be difficult to work for, if you perform, he can make things happen in your career. Joe is also a runner, having competed in several marathons. He tells the story of being denied access to run in the Boston Marathon only to produce a bloody shoe from the New York City Marathon to convince the gatekeepers he was worthy. They let him run.

Joe was viewed as high potential, and AT&T placed him in the Sloan Fellows Program at MIT. (As an aside, he later sponsored Steve Jacobsen to also become a Sloan Fellow.) The educational experience brought business concepts to Joe that would serve him well, such as game theory. Joe was also an instinctual person with a strong bias for action. Joe always had several initiatives working, and many more ideas churning. He obviously was oriented to achieve results. Failure was not an option. Joe also had a great sense of humor; it wasn't self-deprecating, but he could crack you up. He reminds me of Dennis Miller with a rapid-fire, stream-of-consciousness delivery and intellectually rich content. He could also use these same traits to point out what an idiot you were and often did so publicly. His critiques could be colored with profanity, using his best New York City inflections.

Joe was a vice-president in AT&T's Business Markets Group. At the time, AT&T had placed its largest and most valuable accounts into a new offering referred to as Tariff 12, its regulatory designation. The FCC regulatory regime allowed each of these Tariff 12 customers to escape their contract under a program called: "Fresh Look". This was an extraordinary opportunity to lose AT&T's most important customers. Joe organized a team to work with national account managers and was personally involved in negotiations with the customers.

The results were astonishing and far exceeded expectations for retaining these customers. My first encounter with Joe was right after "Fresh Look" was complete. We held a meeting in San Jose, CA. (That was the branch I reported to while stationed in the Sacramento outpost). At AT&T, it was extremely rare for lower level managers to meet directly with senior executives. It was understood only softball questions were permitted. I recall us discussing the rapidly changing regulatory environment in a small group of sales and support managers. He reached forward and grabbed a cookie, broke it in half, and said, "If I'm going to talk about them, I need something sweet in my mouth".

He was very engaging and instilled a sense of urgency. He was not like any other AT&T high-level executive I had met or seen in action. Joe was the antithesis of the CEO at the time: Robert E. Allen. Mr. Allen was a soft spoken, bland, and deliberate man who looked like Mr. Rogers (of the eponymous children's TV show). Joe was promoted to head AT&T's Consumer Long Distance Business, becoming one of the youngest to run a major AT&T operating unit. AT&T's consumer unit was engaged in a multi-front war with MCI and others at this time. MCI was rapidly taking market share. Joe moved quickly and stopped the share losses; he actually reversed the trend to reclaim market share back from MCI. It was extraordinary. Joe was also customer focused and invested heavily in improving the customer experience. I recall the unit received the Malcom Baldridge National Quality Award for these efforts.

The long distance wars were being fought on television with huge advertising campaigns. MCI had edgy campaigns that featured the irreverent and funny Joan Rivers, and tough guy Burt Lancaster. Sprint was converting its network from microwave to fiber optics and unleashed its "Pin Drop" campaign. AT&T relied on the trustworthy and comfortable celebrity of Cliff Robertson as its spokesperson. The advertising strategy evolved and at times included AT&T employees. (While I did get an audition, I did not make the cut. I did, however, receive a coffee mug from McCann-Erickson, our ad agency.) In one forgettable campaign, Joe did the voice-over for one of the most poorly received Super Bowl ads in history, touting the new long distance "iPlan." I'm not sure anyone even understood what the ad was about. It certainly did not compare to Steve Jobs' launch of the iPhone!

While Joe enjoyed great success, his style was in contrast to the staid and reserved management at AT&T. It was obvious his style precluded him from consideration for the CEO role to succeed Robert Allen, as their personalities could not have been more different. Mr. Allen convinced the board to hire an outsider as his successor. As it turned out, Mr. Allen's choice for successor was a disaster.

One of the most influential telecom analysts on Wall Street was Jack Grubman—a former AT&T executive, then working with the great Saloman Smith Barney. Grubman introduced Joe to Qwest founder, Phillip F. Anschutz, in a hangar at the Teterboro Airport. The timing was perfect for all parties.

Joe was brought in to take what was then a construction company to commanding heights in the exploding telecom sector. He was an instant rock star. The company with a quirky name created massive buzz with Joe's arrival and credibility as a heavyweight contender. Joe moved quickly. The company instantly evolved into a player with the lowest cost structure, deploying the newest technology, and ushering in a broad array of new services with the highest reliability. That was the pitch anyway. In short, newer is better on many dimensions, and the old guard was stuck in a high cost model, which left them strategically disadvantaged. Qwest became a darling of Wall Street, and Joe was highly sought after for his stinging, yet humorous, commentary.

I do believe that the break-up of the Bell System, and the opening of the markets it participated in, was a major contributor to our economic growth, increasing productivity, and rising incomes across wide swaths of society. The deregulation under the Clinton Administration was instrumental to the rapid growth of the sector. It was also a significant contributor to the technical leadership this country enjoys in communications, Internet services, computing, software, analytics, and many other operations. It has been as transformational as the intercontinental railroads were in their time. This makes a good argument for a light touch by regulators, and the rate of change is quickening now.

Working for Joe was demanding. As he commuted to Denver from New Jersey, working all night was de rigueur; he had nothing else to do. He was so strong-willed that it was impossible for him to accept why something could not be made to happen. It was as if because he *willed* it to be done, it *shall* be done.

As an example, Qwest sponsored an annual international golf event outside Denver. Joe hated golf and thought golfers were slackers. He did not play much golf. Yet, he chose to play in the pro-am: once with Ernie Els and once with Phil Mickelson, thinking he could will his way to play well. He did not.

He was complex when it came to people, too. When someone did not meet expectations, he would call for them ("go wake them up," he would say) so they could to explain why they fell short to the management team. Yet, he was reluctant to personally fire those same underperformers, and instead relied on Tom Mathews or Afshin Mohebbi to do the deed. Joe would hold meetings where there were many participants and rail-birds (these are people who sit on the sidelines, add no value, and shit on everyone else). The meetings were referred to as "The Joe Show." Presenters spent days preparing for this time and were expected to present business plans, projections, and forecasts, and then discuss results. Joe referred to these inquisitions as "Stump the Stars;" rarely did one leave unscathed. These affairs went late into the night on many occasions. Sometimes, the process was so convoluted a presenter was thrown off their presentation by Joe jumping around to other pages. There were times when the presenter never got passed the first two pages. When someone was failing, Joe would clear the room of the underlings and rail-birds and dress down the loser. That process was referred to as, "The rats jumping ship."

A Bloomberg terminal sat outside of Joe's office. The executives would gather and watch the market quotes and contrast them with Qwest's meteoric rise in value. On occasion, meetings would be disrupted by events (such as GTE's $30 billion offer to acquire MCI) and the executives would go to the Bloomberg terminal and discuss the price movements of the sector's stock prices. Clearly, there was a fixation on valuation, Qwest's and others in the space.

Joe, using his instincts and business savvy, went about transforming Qwest into a significant player in the industry with a market capitalization reaching $100 billion. Joe also displayed an undeniable appetite for mergers and acquisitions. This activity started small with the likes of Colorado Supernet and ICON CMT, on to much bigger game such as LCI International. Joe's tour de force was the US WEST acquisition when he outmaneuvered Global Crossing in what was a hostile transaction. With that transaction, Joe had some explaining to do: "Why would a rebellious Internet-oriented start-up acquire a dinosaur like US West"? His answer was prescient: "Cash flow."

Joe was unimpressed with the management members at US West and many of them beat a hasty retreat for the exits. This included their CEO, Sol Trujillo. Mr. Trujillo's public rhetoric upon his exit was quite harsh. Greener pastures would await Mr. Trujillo at Orange in France (despite speaking no French) and at the Australian telecom, Telstra. Mr. Trujillo seemed to have been given a pass for his failed strategies at US West, which included selling its wireless business (New Vector) and investing in PC retailing and real estate.

Joe was relentless in his pursuit of revenue and earnings growth. He always had been. However, the challenge to grow rapidly was exponentially more difficult when you just acquired a business with much larger revenues, which were stagnant or shrinking, and dwarfed your own growth segments. It was perceived by many that Joe perpetuated a "culture of fear" to make the numbers.

I was involved in a number of conversations regarding revenue and projected revenue. I was asked to join Afshin Mohebbi's Operations Committee. Afshin had joined the company recently as its president and chief operating officer. Afshin maintained a list of "initiatives." These were short-term revenue opportunities that could potentially occur in the current quarter. Many of these initiatives involved the sale of IRUs: large dollar sales of fiber optic capacity.

These transactions were at the heart of the Qwest accounting issues. Greg Casey led the sales organization that dealt with these sales. I thought it odd, but he was reluctant to discuss the details and timing of these transactions in this group, despite its being convened for that specific purpose. Greg was intimately involved in the negotiation of these transactions. Now we know why he was reluctant to discuss them as these were the fatal transactions. Joe was aware these deals were "hairy" as they were both quarter closing and non-recurring.

The internal issue these sales created was centered on disclosing to the investing public that as much as 10% of revenues were non-recurring. At issue, were the materiality of the deals and the company's transparency of its revenue streams. It is my understanding that Arthur Andersen provided guidance that said, "If less than 10% of total revenues are non-recurring, they need not be broken out separately." This is the question of materiality. Additionally, this revenue was classified as: "Data and IP" (Internet), which suggested outsized revenue growth in areas most highly valued by Wall Street (transparency). Virtually all revenue from these transactions was recorded at the time of sale with only a small portion recognized ratably for maintenance.

As the market for IRUs dried up, a series of transactions were concocted that allegedly had no economic value. They were referred to as, "round trippers," where Qwest would sell $100 million to Global Crossing and they would sell $100 million to Qwest simultaneously. I can't affirm that Joe knew of these round-trip deals. He assuredly knew that IRU transactions were used to close the quarter and, "make the numbers." It was also alleged that side deals were constructed to obfuscate the terms from finance and accounting, and preserve the recognition of revenue. I don't believe Joe knew of these, but I can't say definitively as I was not present.

This suggests some turned a blind eye to get a deal done, even if red lines were crossed. One could devise a rationale to support the transactions as my superiors testified to in their SEC depositions. I saw no direct evidence of sales back dating contracts, but there were rumors of, "36 day months." I recall hearing Joe berate his management team about too much reliance on and frustration with non-recurring revenues. I did hear Joe remark about these IRUs, that, "They happen with such regularity, maybe they are recurring revenues." There is no denying rumors of these type of transactions placed the company under intense scrutiny. The pressure began to mount from Wall Street for more clarity on the opaque numbers.

As this was occurring, Joe received a new employment contract. People were outraged that the board of directors was rewarding him for what appeared to be financial irregularities, at best, and, perhaps, criminal conduct. Joe's new contract was said to be worth $250 million. Typical of Joe, he said, "I create more economic value than a shortstop" (referring to Alex Rodriquez's new contract he signed with the Texas Rangers worth the same amount).

There were many at US West who hated Joe. They didn't like his brashness. After the fall of the house of Qwest, the stock value in their retirement plans plummeted. I do recall Joe quickly resolving potential labor dispute issues with the unions and moved quickly to renew their labor agreements. I also know that many of the technicians were scrounging for tools and parts and some were hoarding valuable ones. Joe personally directed initiatives and resources to solve those problems. I believe these issues were resolved on Joe's watch.

AS THE INVESTIGATION into Qwest's accounting practices grew more intense, the board forced Joe out. He left a rich man, but he was facing both civil and criminal actions. After an exhaustive review of the accounting, reporting, and revenue recognition practices at Qwest, Joe was charged with criminal insider trading. Joe went on trial in Denver, obviously a hostile venue for him based on the press coverage, which was non-stop. His change of venue motion was denied.

He employed renowned lawyer Herb Stern who, for a reported fee of $75 million, did not put on much of a case, calling only three witnesses in his defense. Joe's defense rested on the future contracts Qwest was to receive from the government's National Security apparatus. This testimony was denied airing for national security reasons. Thus, the lynchpin of Joe's defense was emasculated. Later, the NSA indicated that the contracts Joe believed would have delivered the revenue and profits that buttressed his public forecasts were illusory. Joe claimed that the contracts were scuttled as retribution for failing to agree to government initiatives for monitoring Qwest customers in the post-9/11 environment.

Joe was convicted at trial on 19 of 42 insider-trading counts. He was required to pay fines of $19 million and disgorge $52 million of ill-gotten gains. He was also sentenced to six years in prison. He did not take the stand in his defense. After losing his appeal, Joe was sent to prison. I spoke with him via telephone prior to his incarceration. He was very feisty and angry. I'm not sure he fully understood what awaited him. I'm not sure any of us would be prepared to enter the Federal prison system.

During his incarceration, I exchanged letters with him, usually one per month. I wrote him in attempt to keep his spirits high and for him to stay positive. His wife, Anne, included me in emails she sent, which provided updates about Joe and his family and Joe's own writings. His letters to me were short and handwritten on blue-lined paper. He described the awful conditions of the prison system. The food was worse than terrible. He was given a plastic "spork" to eat a pork chop. It was freezing and he slept in everything he had, including a stocking cap. His clothing and shoes would have been rejected if donated to the Salvation Army.

His contemporaries did not share his interest in Russian history, Existentialism, or other books he read, which numbered well over one hundred. He was able to work out and stay in good shape. He wrote of mentoring other inmates, teaching GED courses, breaking up fights, and dealing with the anxiety that comes from living in such a harsh place with many insane people. I also understand Joe delivered the Eucharist to other inmates. He shared how criminals made their lives worse by smuggling in drugs, pornography, and other bad behavior. He wrote of the friends he made and how he survived the ordeal by being streetwise, funny, and tough as nails.

What a contrast for a man who lived in a beautiful home, flew in private jets, and garnered an adoring press following. I had dinner at his home after he paid his debt to society. It was a beautiful steak: a bone-in New York. Eating in jail must have been an experience; I could tell by the way he guarded his plate with his arm and sat at the end of the table on the edge of his chair. He showed us some of his prized possessions in his home office. Near the photograph of him shaking hands with President Bush (W) during his tenure as head of the National Security Telecommunications Advisory Committee, was a shot of him in the joint in his jail garb, posing with his mate "Spoonie."

The jury determined Joe's actions deserved incarceration. Not many of those at Qwest who he'd made rich were interested in taking the stand in his defense. A couple took the stand to testify against him. I don't know if a different defense attorney could have produced an alternative outcome by putting on a more substantive case. I did hear an attorney remark he could have, "...gotten the same result for only half the money." The specific accounting allegations discussed previously were never put to trial.

I realize that many employees were laid off, but that was going to happen over time anyway. The Qwest/US West merger rationale included the elimination of positions that were duplicative. These are the synergies that accrue to shareowners in all mergers. The industry was experiencing tectonic changes that eventually eliminated whole lines of business. I realize that some people lost money on the company's stock, but the whole technology sector was an inflated bubble. Qwest did not go bankrupt.

Many believe the issues that arose during this time were solely related to greed: pump the stock by using funky deals, and then dump the stock to get rich. I was never under the impression greed motivated Joe. I think Joe was motivated to make AT&T pay for not promoting him to the top job. Joe wanted to take market share from AT&T and grow Qwest from nothing to something, and the valuation would follow naturally. For a brief moment in time that did happen and a print ad was created urging AT&T to pick on someone its own size, closing with the line, "Oh, I guess you did," and showing each company's market capitalization at $100 Billion. The ad never ran but it did capture the emotion.

Joe was not a flashy dresser despite once wearing a Brioni suit at the infamous US West integration meeting where he arrived on horseback. (Phil had a custom saddle made for Joe for the event) Joe did not engage in conspicuous consumption, although he had an affinity for Porsches. Still, despite his wealth, he purchased a used one. When discussing the purchase of his Porsche with Bill Redderson of BellSouth, Joe complained of the turn signal not working properly ("the clicker" he called it). Mr. Redderson replied;

"Hell Joe, you could buy Porsche [the company]." (I am unsure what Alex Rodriquez was driving at the time.)

I know Joe felt that stock prices of those in the sector were overvalued when there was talk of a potential merger with Winstar. Joe said, "They want us to use our inflated currency to buy their inflated currency." As it turns out, he was right when the tech bubble burst and we all crashed.

For me, I'm conflicted. Joe, reluctantly, provided me opportunities at the leading edge of the Internet's inception. My team and I got to change the world, arguably for the better. We had fun, too.

On the other hand, I had my reputation destroyed by the SEC litigation. I feel like I could have continued to make a positive impact for a business and its employees. The fact of the litigation denied me that opportunity. As I heard from even members of my own family, "Where there's smoke, there's fire." The allegation alone is sufficient proof of wrongdoing (we'll explore this later). The allegation alone is enough to end one's career.

SEVEN

philip f. anschutz — the man with the midas touch...

PHILIP F. ANSCHUTZ is an amazing guy. He is an amazing businessman.

The legend begins with the story of his first deal in the oil patch where he acquired a couple of oil wells. Upon consummating the transaction in Wyoming, he returned to Denver where the television news was reporting a couple of oil wells were on fire. It turned out that these wells were the ones Mr. Anschutz had just acquired. The person you called to put out oil well fires was the legendary Red Adair. Mr. Anschutz placed a call to Red Adair who said, "You don't have the money to pay me, kid." Legend has it that Mr. Anschutz was aware of a film under consideration by one of the Hollywood studios called *Hellfighters* starring (appropriately) John Wayne playing Red Adair. Mr. Anschutz then called the studio and sold them the rights to film Red Adair actually putting out the fire on his oil wells; he used the proceeds from the movie rights deal to pay Mr. Adair for his services.

Later, Mr. Anschutz acquired a ranch that held large reserves of oil. It was reported Mobil acquired the rights for the oil for $500 million and agreed to pay Mr. Anschutz a 17% royalty on the remainder of what was pumped form the property. In 1982, $500 million was a lot of money. In 1984, Mr. Anschutz acquired the Rio Grande Railroad, which later was the vehicle used to acquire the Southern Pacific Railroad (SP). I understand the rail operations never made money, but SP held a vast amount of real estate that was sold off to pay down the debt owed by the company. Subsequently, the rail operation was sold to Union Pacific Railway.

With the SP acquisition, Mr. Anschutz also acquired a vast trove of Western art that he curated himself. It is rumored to be the single largest collection of Western art; Frederick Remington is prominent in his collection. He also acquired a number of private rail cars, beautiful flatware, sterling silver service items, and a number of interesting antiques hearkening back to the days of the robber barons. These amazing artifacts are a wonderful homage to our country's earlier days and our entry into the industrial age.

One of the SP entities was SP Construction, which was initially involved in erecting microwave communications facilities along the railroad's rights-of-way. Prior to the advent of fiber optics, the new carriers relied on microwave. Sprint developed the largest microwave network and MCI was an acronym for Microwave Communications, Inc. During Mr. Anschutz' ownership, the company developed new technology that was known as a "rail plow." This was pure genius. A device was outfitted on the locomotive and used to dig the trench the conduit pipe would be laid in through which the fiber optic cables would be run. The rail plow locomotive pulled cars that carried the conduit on reels and could lay down conduit more rapidly and cost-effectively than any other method. Alongside the rail tracks, buildings known as ROW huts (or Right-of-Way), could be placed to house the electronics required to light the fiber optics.

It is an interesting intersection that both the cornerstone of our Westward expansion and entry into the Industrial Age relied on the railroads. In the twentieth century, they provided the bedrock in which the critical infrastructure of the Internet age—fiber optics—was laid.

Telecommunications was and is a capital-intensive business, and new players were seeking to gain a technical and cost advantage. Fiber optics along rail lines were an ideal match as they had the additional benefit of being less susceptible to impairments due to construction activity and weather events. It should be noted that telegraph lines were placed along the rail lines at the advent of long distance communications. SP Construction (later known as Qwest Construction Services) began to enter into contracts with major players, including MCI, GTE, and Frontier Communications. Mr. Anschutz brilliantly seized the opportunity. While the trench was open, why not put in a conduit for his future use? The cost was virtually zero as the others paid for the direct construction costs. Pure genius.

SP Telecom was an entity under the SP umbrella that was marketing communications services. SP Telecom acquired a microwave-based service provider whose antennae were located along the rail lines. The founder of that network picked a whimsical name that he felt was quixotic and captured the spirit of the yin and yang. SP Telecom later adopted that name. That name was Qwest.

Qwest for Truth ...and Change

I met Mr. Anschutz on a couple of occasions. When I interviewed for the position, Steve Jacobsen told me, "Phil is an asset flipper," clearly indicating Qwest was being built to be sold rather than being built to last.

I had my first encounter with Mr. Anschutz at the old Mile High stadium, attending a Colorado Rapids soccer game, in the owner's suite. The old stadium was far from plush. Mr. Anschutz was wearing blue jeans and drank a Coors beer from the bottle. He is a cigar man, but only enjoys them unlit. He was known as the father of Major League Soccer in the US and owned more than one team. He was very approachable and I asked him about his development project in Los Angeles, which would later be the home of the NBA's Los Angeles Lakers and Clippers, as well as the LA Kings hockey team. He told me that the project had been approved that very day. He seemed blasé about its approval. The development would later expand to include LA Live, the Microsoft Theater, a Ritz Carlton hotel, and a number of restaurants and other retail outlets. It was the cornerstone of the downtown Los Angeles' redevelopment effort.

Later, while I was writing a memo to Mr. Anschutz (not under my signature, of course) as to why the Staples Center in Los Angeles would not be called the Qwest Center, I was told, "Phil is a simple man, keep it simple."

On another occasion, I had the opportunity to ride in his private rail cars from Denver to the Winter Park ski resort. There were three private rail cars attached to the commercial cars, carrying skiers to Winter Park; one was a bubble top, one a food service car, and finally the caboose. It was a special journey as I could imagine how the robber barons travelled back during Wild West times. The guests were a mix of employees and customers and Mr. Anschutz' guests included the singer, Seal. I guess this was a precursor to the formation of the Anschutz Entertainment Group (AEG) and AEG Live. I was introduced to Mr. Anschutz as we headed back to Denver in the luxuriously appointed caboose, and he indicated, "I know who Rick is." He was very comfortable to talk with, and we discussed technology and wireless communications while Seal took a nap (he had a long day on a snowboard, apparently). We discussed text messaging. At the time, we used Blackberry devices that had yet to be integrated with the phone. We discussed the convergence of device technology where phones and texting would be on a single device along with other capabilities and how that would dramatically change the landscape.

I was trying to impress him with my background in wireless. Of course, none of us saw what Apple was about to unleash on the world. We saw cellphones as a mobile telephone; Steve Jobs saw mobile computing devices that ran applications, including *an app that is a phone*. Mr. Anschutz was comfortable on a range of topics. I was in the presence of a shrewd, capable, and brilliant business magnate. He is *not* "a simple man."

One important question in the Qwest debacle is how much did Mr. Anschutz know about the quality of the revenues being reported? On the Qwest board sat trusted Anschutz associates, Cy Harvey and Craig Slater from the Anschutz Company, as well as Mr. Anschutz himself. As the board of directors met, did they have a thorough understanding of how the company's growth was occurring? Were board members conversant with the accounting issues raised by the SEC in its litigation? I did not prepare materials for board meetings nor did I attend any of them. I believe this points to the fallacy of the composition of the members of boards of directors. What does Marilyn Carlson Nelson (Travel and Hospitality) know about telecommunications? Or Linda Alvarado (Construction)? Or Tom Donohue (US Chamber of Commerce)? All were members of the board during the time in question, and all were obviously outsiders. Activists want independent outsiders on company boards. Can independent board members synthesize the complexity of an unfamiliar business? Unlike MCI (or Enron), no members of the board, except for Joe Nacchio, were implicated.

According to the SEC complaint, from the middle of 1999 into 2002 there was a lack of transparency regarding the composition of Qwest's recurring versus non-recurring revenues. Additionally, the SEC allegation asserted that many transactions were recorded but were contemporaneous with other telecom companies and served no economic interest or purpose. This suggests that the board, including Mr. Anschutz, were either unable to detect these purported irregularities or unable to recognize them. Additionally, the US West employees assigned to perform the due diligence prior to the merger of the two companies were unable to uncover these irregularities. Remember, we are talking about $3.8 billion here. If this is the case, then either the board, the US West teams, outside consultants, and Wall Street dealmakers were incompetent and were not able to understand the business, or had some motivation to look past these issues. Another possibility is that the heads of the various business units made their presentations believable while obfuscating the actual trajectory of the business. Finally, this implicates the impartial view and acceptance of the honesty of the numbers, which were validated by Arthur Andersen, the accounting firm in Qwest's regulatory filings.

These elements raise a number of issues, including:
- Do individual board members from outside the business have the time to really understand and peel back the façade to understand quality of revenue issues?
- Do outsiders really have the expertise to evaluate a business that is very different from theirs?
- Should board members have a financial stake in the firm?
- Should board members be subject to personal liability as was the case in the MCI Worldcom litigation?
- What resources should be made available to the Board of Directors to better understand the real workings inside the company?

In the examination of these issues, we need to look at what motivates the various stakeholders:
- Sales makes its numbers and gets paid
- Qwest management makes its numbers and gets rewarded in both cash and accelerated stock vesting with the merger with US West
- US West management gets to close the merger and accelerate vesting of their stock options under the Change of Control provisions
- Arthur Andersen helps a client make its numbers and pushes the envelope on accounting to do so
- Success at Arthur Andersen creates opportunities for its consulting arm, Andersen Consulting (now Accenture)
- Industry analysts become participants as market values soar, and merger and acquisition activity increases
- Qwest board members ride the wave, which is personally lucrative

Qwest for Truth ...and Change

I'm not suggesting some grand conspiracy was at work here. Things were moving rapidly and the industry was attracting incredible valuations and generating vast wealth for its participants. Perhaps events were moving too quickly for a more sober assessment of the quality of revenues. I would posit that it is easy to see alignment among the stakeholders, and that various forms of pressure create a strong desire to not disappoint.

In all the merger transactions that Qwest entered into during my tenure, Philip Anschutz' holdings were diluted. He did not act like an "asset flipper." His actions appeared to be directed to growing a more substantial enterprise.

I am a capitalist. Capitalism does have some ugly aspects. Greed is one of them. Robber Barons indeed.

Caricature of Phil Anschutz and his business interests

Courtesy of the New York Times

EIGHT
corporate culture

ONE OF MY FAVORITE business books is *Built to Last* written by Jim Collins and Jerry Porras. The book examines the characteristics of companies that have long-lasting performance as compared to their peers. One of the many examples of these great companies' attributes relates to their corporate culture. Rather than being created by a visionary founder, as is the obvious case of Steve Jobs and Apple (and perhaps a once in a generation occurrence), most great companies do not start with a visionary product or founder. Instead, an environment is created where individuals are permitted to explore and create products without the fear of being fired. Failure is an expected outcome when new concepts are being explored. Additionally, a culture is created that embraces a bit of chaos; employees are engaged at a high level, fervently believing their ideas and the company can and will change the world. Through the unrelenting churn of business cycles, these companies maintain and even enhance their core ideology. The authors describe how this unique *esprit de corps* forms a culture that leads to excellence that is sustained over time. *Built to Last* is a terrific read. I enthusiastically recommend it.

My experiences in corporate America were remarkably different based upon how dissimilar their corporate cultures were.

AT&T

AT&T is one of the most historic and important companies ever. Its genesis dates to Alexander Graham Bell who invented the ability to transmit his voice over distance, which he patented on March 7, 1876. As the technology came into commercial use for telephone networks, many independent companies were formed. In some cases, there were several telephone companies vying for the same customer. This overlap was inefficient (think of multiple companies wiring every house and building). Theodore Vail came along with the idea of rolling up the independent telephone operators to reach scale and eliminate redundancy. The organizing principle was deemed "Universal Service" in which the Bell System would endeavor to deliver telephone service to every household in America. The underlying economic theory was that AT&T should be a monopoly, without any competition, so that the costs of serving rural America could be subsidized by the profits generated in more populous areas.

There existed a legendary figure who played a prominent role in the development of and fervent nature of AT&T's culture. The legend comes from an employee named Angus Macdonald who stood sentinel during a blizzard in 1888, ensuring the operation of the main line connecting Boston and New York City continued. The image and effect of maintaining extremely reliable telecommunications became the hallmark of AT&T. The employee recognition program was birthed from this act. The award was dubbed the Spirit of Service.

Angus MacDonald

telcomhistory.org

Qwest for Truth ...and Change

AT&T became a vertically integrated company that manufactured all the components used to deliver telephone and data services: switching stations, wire, telephone sets, business systems, transmission equipment, and even telephone poles. The company operated the Bell Laboratories that was an unparalleled engine of innovation, including these blockbusters: the transistor; the laser, Unix (a derivative of which runs on your iPhone); programming languages C and C++; the charged coupled device (CCD) that is a semiconductor image sensor (also on your iPhone); as well as synchronized motion pictures (the Talkie). The many other contributions to science, statistics, engineering, and technology are too numerous to list here.

As a side note, Apple founders Steve Jobs and Steve Wozniak began their partnership as "Phone Phreaks," building and selling "Blue Boxes" designed to bypass the billing system of AT&T so the user could make free calls. Thus, the foundation of that partnership was made through their collaboration in developing and selling an illegal product.

Steve Jobs and Steve Wozniak in 1975 with a "Blue Box."

In operation, the Bell System was ubiquitous across the nation. There were other independent telephone operators, but none compared in scope and size to AT&T. AT&T had become pervasive, and telephone service was affordable and available in virtually all of America. As a vertically integrated company that manufactured all the components used in delivering service, protecting the network was of paramount importance, as well as preserving its economic framework via its monopoly status. The network could not be "contaminated" by allowing any device not manufactured by AT&T to be connected to it. In 1962, the Carterfone decision enabled a "foreign attachment" to be connected to the Bell System's network. It was a simple telephone, but it represented the introduction of competition to AT&T's monopoly. Over time, others came along, most notably MCI, to further challenge the wisdom of granting AT&T a monopoly.

The government eventually sued AT&T on antitrust grounds beginning in 1974. The litigation dragged on for years. It was expensive and a distraction to management. (Government litigation is characterized by its ability to have no limits in terms of time or resources.) In 1982, AT&T agreed to break itself up based on the calculation that it would be free to enter the computing business after divesting itself of the telephone companies. The decision was made by then CEO Charlie Brown (who was later succeeded by Jimmy Olson, serious men with the names of cartoon characters).

It was a wrenching decision internally and was counter to the organizing principle of "Universal Service." I saw Mr. Brown playing golf at the Crosby Pro-Am at Pebble Beach (on the Spyglass Hill course), which would later become the AT&T Pebble Beach National Pro-Am. Mr. Brown was monotone in his dark tan slacks and brown cardigan sweater with the sleeves rolled up a bit. I could see in Mr. Brown's demeanor and gait, the toll of his decision; he seemed joyless and spent.

At the time of divestiture, AT&T employed over one million people, generated $110 billion in revenues, and $7 billion in profits. The company was an American icon noted for its steady performance and ability to pay dividends; it was dubbed the "widows' and orphans' stock."

The company appeared to be totally unprepared for divestiture. I began my career working in the unregulated telephone equipment subsidiary known as American Bell, Inc. (ABI), which would also house the Computer Systems Division. The development effort for telephone systems was obviously centered on large businesses. The company had just introduced the System 85, which was only for large enterprises. At the time, the vast majority of the equipment customers used was rented to them. Much of AT&T's telephone technology was dated and a clutch of competitors entered the market with new, high tech systems. ABI was caught flat-footed with electro-mechanical systems that were complicated, expensive, and a generation behind. In addition, the sales organization, reared in a monopoly environment, more resembled order-takers than a professional sales force (apologies to my former colleagues who are offended).

ABI was launched with $5.5 billion to last for its first five years as it ramped up sales volumes by replacing the rental equipment revenues with sales of new gear. It wasn't even close to breaking even and burned through the cash in three and one-half years. The gruesome task of force reductions would begin.

I recall a story of an AT&T executive by the name of William Ellingshaus being somewhat dismayed by AT&T's slow start in the computing business. He said, "We thought we knew as much about processors as anyone." The problem was AT&T wasn't selling processors, it was intending to compete with IBM, who provided the most critical and strategic information technology solutions at the time. Interestingly, AT&T had erected a new world headquarters

**AT&T Headquarters
550 Madison Avenue, New York, NY
(Now the Sony Building)**

Qwest for Truth ...and Change

at 550 Madison in Manhattan directly across the street from IBM's world headquarters. It was slated to be the titanic clash for the ages. The AT&T building was amazing! Golden Boy (also known as the Spirit of Communication) had been relocated from the old building at 195 Broadway and placed in the three-story lobby at 550 Madison. There were outdoor spaces for people to socialize. The top of the building had a unique design and was dubbed a "High-boy Chippendale." I had the opportunity to visit the building once and was impressed by the high ceilings and the luxurious long-pile wool carpeting. It was sometimes referred to as, "The tombstone of the Bell System." It is now the Sony Building. Golden Boy has been relocated to AT&T's new headquarters in Dallas, Texas.

AT&T Spirit of Communication— Golden Boy

I recall the Computer Systems management team telling the sales organization if any of their customers had an IBM System 36 or System 38 they should get them to consider the (dashingly named) 3B line of UNIX computers we were selling. The only issue was that the 3B line had no applications library to run, which is kind of important when you are selling solutions to a client.

After the divestiture, I transferred from American Bell (ABI) to AT&T Communications (renamed from AT&T Long Lines), which handled long distance and data services. This portion of the business was the cash cow. To identify sales quotas for each sales team, which consisted of an account executive (sales) and a systems consultant (network design, billing issues, problem solver), a process occurred where the sales teams would present their understanding of the accounts they were responsible for. These presentations included: what their revenues were; what growth or decline could be expected; who the decision makers were, and what services they were using. AT&T's equipment and long-distance sales teams were not allowed to collaborate, thus there was a duplication of sales teams. The AT&T Communications teams enjoyed recurring revenues and were expected to develop deep relationships with clients. The ABI sales teams were more transactional. Since I was a rookie, I was asked to perform a staff role and help organize the sales team's presentations to the branch manager. I was incredulous over the presentations where seasoned sales teams would come in and say their accounts had suffered no competitive losses of revenue. At the end of this process, the sales teams' projections were rolled up and submitted by the branch to the area, then the region. It was a bit of a charade because there was little room for negotiation. The HQ staff had already assigned a number to the region, which was allocated to the area and then to the branches.

I think this example is valuable in gaining an insight into AT&T's corporate culture. There were many, many layers of management. I recall hearing that at Western Electric (the manufacturing arm, later named Lucent) there were 57 layers of management. I don't know if that's true, but I'm sure it felt that way. The management staff had almost a regal aura to them. They were certainly insulated from the action in the streets. The desire was, in part, to shield senior management from bad news. Only good news traveled up the chain. There were huge staff organizations, many creating work for each other rather than adding value to the front-line, customer-facing work groups. When I visited headquarters at 295 N. Maple Avenue in Basking Ridge, New Jersey (now owned by Verizon), I understood there to be 20,000 employees housed in that one building. It was a city unto itself.

The output of the staff that I saw included an unwieldy sales compensation plan that was usually delivered in March. The sales compensation plan was *the* definitive statement by management about what products and services were most important: "sell these to maximize your income." This was accompanied with plans from the Industry Marketing Group and provided ideas as to what products were relevant to particular markets (for example, forest products companies, wholesalers, or manufacturing companies). The concept was that account executives would have expertise in their industry, much like our friends at IBM, and would be invited to participate in client corporate strategy development. This was laughable, yet it was the foundation of the career path of sales executives. All were required to demonstrate their industry sales expertise by making a "systems sale" that changed the way a company did business using AT&T products, as described earlier. Sales executives were being brought in from outside the company to imbue a sales culture;

many were recruited from IBM. This too was a wrenching change for veterans of the monopoly culture. Oddly, the distribution of quota (or sales and revenue targets) was socialized. That is to say, quota was taken away from under-performers and given to over-performers to smooth out the bell curve. There seemed to be an implicit desire to make everyone's performance "acceptable."

Every area of AT&T's business that remained after divestiture was under fierce attack by numerous competitors. Morphing from a monopoly to fully competitive businesses meant market share erosion was inevitable. (At divestiture, the Bell Companies retained their monopoly local telephone services, and AT&T relinquished to the Bells the cellular and the Yellow Pages businesses. AT&T retained manufacturing and long distance, and was freed to enter the computing business.)

It didn't take long to realize that the company urgently needed to reduce the number of employees. AT&T employment was generally considered to be career for one's entire working life. As previously mentioned, there were many employees working well after their 30th anniversary working at AT&T. (I remember being asked when I was a new employee "how much time I had?" When I responded less than a year, the reply was, "I have more time than that in the men's room.") When your culture is based on a spirit of service and tenure is highly valued, what process do you use to resize your staff? With socialized quota setting, it made sales results less prominent and subjective factors more important. The company implemented rankings based on a bell curve that included a variety of factors. The bell curve required "forced rankings" and the bottom 10% were targeted for dismissal. This was a brutal undertaking as dreams of life-long, secure careers were shattered. Additionally, the affected employees were to be told prior to Thanksgiving about their demise with the statement: "You have been targeted and will be off payroll effective 1/1," (which meant January first) ... Happy Holidays!

I REMEMBER TAKING A CLIENT to Pebble Beach Golf Links for the golf event after AT&T replaced the Crosby family, and became the title sponsor. It was a beautiful affair, sitting in the hospitality tent along the first fairway that was connected to an amazing home. The tables were large, covered with beautiful white linens and flower arrangements. Large spectacular flower arrangements hung from the ceiling of the tent and both indoor and outdoor seating was available. The food was amazing, and formally attired wait staff made the rounds with Mimosas, Bloody Mary's, and Ramos fizzes. Several PGA Tour professionals mingled with the guests: Fuzzy Zoeller, Chip Beck, Ben Crenshaw, and others. From Hollywood, Cliff Robertson, who was AT&T's principle television spokesperson, was present. What was odd was that the AT&T executives huddled amongst themselves. The only executive I saw mingling with clients was Vittorio Cassoni from the newly acquired Olivetti Company, designed to aid the computer system division's efforts. I was from sales, so I was naturally disappointed the executives did not mingle with our customers.

There was a cultural defect, in my view, which was detrimental to having better market, organizational, and competitive landscape perspectives. AT&T was level conscious. This meant you were to know your place; interaction was limited to your immediate manager. If you were ever in a forum with senior management, it was verboten to speak, and if you did, you were expected to be nice. No bad news. No hard questions. There was an occasional "skip-level" meeting. This practice occurred when management in your reporting chain was absent and you were invited to meet with senior management in their place. I recall being invited to one of these in San Francisco at 795 Folsom Street, the regional headquarters. The group consisted of "high-potential" employees, participating in a program where you were to be groomed for additional responsibilities. AT&T's management development strategy was cross-pollination, where you would be exposed to Operations, Finance, Marketing, or any number of other functional areas. Thus, our group was made up of differing functional areas. Our host was a senior officer from New Jersey by the name of John Smart. We gathered in a nice conference room where lunch was served. We were told to wear our suit jackets throughout. Mr. Smart came in, pleasantries were exchanged, and sandwiches were served. I had never observed a sandwich being eaten with a knife and fork, so this was my first experience being in an actual Seinfeld episode (Mr. Peterman used utensils as well, but his meal was a Snickers bar). Much like a Seinfeld episode, this was a meeting about nothing. Nothing of substance was said. Everything was hunky dory, despite getting our butts kicked in the marketplace, and HQ was always interested in some report that was a distraction.

The organization was so large it was unwieldy and uncoordinated. It made it difficult to understand how things worked together and who was responsible. Operational expertise was decentralized and removed from the customer-facing units. As an example, there were massive billing systems. In telecom services, billing capabilities drive customer dissatisfaction and also determine what products and services you can offer and mix together to tighten the customer bond (the Holy Grail was telephone, wireless, and TV on a single bill from your provider, substitute Internet access for telephone today). There was a billing system being developed with over $1 billion invested that was discontinued. It was completely abandoned. ABI was launched with a product known as AIS Net 1000 (AIS meaning Advanced Information Services). Over $1 billion was spent on its development and I can only recall a couple of customers ever being announced as users. AIS Net 1000 was a packet-switched network, which consisted of multiple paths, redundant switches, and various network access points. The network contained its own separate computers that ran proprietary applications. If that sounds to you like the Internet we all use today, it was, except for the closed applications library. Perhaps that was the IBM influence, as their applications were proprietary and rented rather than owned then. Perhaps it was the "we know best mentality" that stems from the "foreign attachment" DNA. These are but two examples in what clearly was a bloated and bureaucratic organization going through a wrenching transition that no amount of planning could have made sense of.

During my time at AT&T, I never witnessed any behavior that bordered on lacking integrity. I was a low-level manager in a remote location far removed from senior management and had no insight as to how financial reporting occurred. In the sales organization, there was a focus on achieving sales results. We spent a great deal of time forecasting sales and reconciling proposals that were pending or lost. I recall Rich Burk commenting on the obsession of "counting things." At AT&T, there were so many people involved across the functional organizations. It was considered a group of checkers busily checking the other checkers who were checking up on the sales groups. I don't think it was possible to fudge a contract date or manipulate an order; the internal controls were too pervasive. There was the culture of the organization where integrity meant everything as well. Under the "Spirit of Service" there was just no room to cut corners, even when you are bleeding customers.

McCAW CELLULAR, INC.

McCaw Cellular, Inc.

At AT&T, I had a customer that was quite large and growing. At first, I was their account executive and later the sales manager responsible for the account. They were the next largest account in the branch after the State of California, which included the University of California and California State University systems. The account was named Cable Data and they provided billing services, and other operational elements for cable television operators. One of their senior executives was a very driven woman by the name of Maggie Wilderotter, who I had interacted with on occasion. (Maggie would later become the Chairman and CEO of Frontier Communications.) It came as a shock when she left Cable Data to become regional president of Cellular One, the marketing name used by McCaw Cellular and others. It was more shocking when she reached out to me to consider joining her in the fledgling cellular business. I began an interview process that was far different than what I expected or experienced at AT&T. I interviewed with the HR person, but that department was called "People Development." I interviewed with members of Maggie's regional staff at multiple levels. The role I was pursuing was not in the regional staff, and I would not be reporting directly to Maggie. I was interviewing for the director of sales and marketing for the district operation. I had interviews with the people who would be reporting to me, some of who were competing for the same job. I interviewed with the functional managers from Customer Care, Billing, Operations, Real Estate, and Engineering. The people I interviewed with collaborated on my selection. The introductions would serve me well later.

I accepted the position. The company was at the time a large start-up. It was a crazy business because customers understood the value of the product and beat a path to our door to get it. We had a single competitor in our market: Pac Tel Cellular. The sales organization was, shall we say, embryonic. The main channel of distribution was a network of authorized dealers. The dealers were compensated on the sale of the phone and wanted no interaction with the customer after for messy things such as billing, equipment problems, and collections. We operated one retail outlet in an industrial park that also managed inventory and distribution of phones (we sold phones to dealers also) and installed phones in vehicles. My task was to build a sales force that would have better and more enduring relationships with the small and medium sized business segment. We also needed to figure out a way to stop punching holes in the gas tanks of Lamborghinis.

THE COMPANY did not have reams of manuals describing operating protocols as AT&T did. The company published a list of goals and values. They were the yardstick everything was measured by. There were less than a dozen and they were simple to understand and live.

Our goal is to establish our company as the premier convenience communications company in the world. To do this, we must earn the continuing loyalty of customers by providing them with network service systems which (sic) they acknowledge to be of superior value in a way which (sic) is profitable to us, thus creating long-term rewards for our shareholders and employees.

Therefore, we will::

1. **Hire and develop great people** (it's the most important thing we do). Decentralize and empower them to make decisions,but balance this to take advantage of our strengths.
2. **Stay close to our customers.** Listen to them and care for them beyond their expectations.
3. **Provide superior network service** systems of the best quality, as defined by the customer.
4. **Pursue excellence in all we do.** It helps make customers happy and gives real meaning to life.
5. **Keep it simple.** Focus on results (satisfying customers), not on form (administrative processes). This will be especially important as we grow.

6. **Run lean** (but spend wisely to achieve our goals and values).
7. **Be humble.** It helps to keep an open mind, a caring attitude, and respect for others.
8. **Be a team player.** Teams are more powerful than individuals.
9. **Employ good judgment.** It makes empowerment work.
10. **Keep our promises.** It builds precious credibility.
11. **Consider the future** (with an eye on the customer).
    Be flexible and open to new ideas and change.
    Be respectfully irreverent, questioning established ways, the "impossible," and things that conflict with our goals and values.

As indicated, these goals and values were the cornerstone of the culture at McCaw. They were visible everywhere. They were simple to understand, but most importantly, they were simple to own. They were constantly referred to in decision-making. They formed the basis of our recognition systems.

It is a real balance to provide superior network services while running lean, but it is a balance that must be struck. After AT&T, you would not be surprised to learn my favorite was, and still is… Keep it simple.

There was a small sales force, and we were busy developing them and growing the staff to serve larger business accounts. It was a bit like putting saddles on wild mustangs and going for a ride. We did a lot of training on sales skills, written proposal development, presentation skills, and account management. There was some resistance to a dress code, but over time they understood that as sales professionals we needed to look the role. The wild mustangs did warm up business attire. It made a difference in their attitude. They looked marvelous.

We spent a lot of time developing the compensation plan. It was important to get the rewards right and to incent the behavior we were seeking. We managed to get the entire plan on two sheets of paper, and eventually included a vacation plan that balanced the needs of the company and our employees. (Sales quotas never go on holiday.)

From a management perspective, we were expected to create our own MBOs and then develop them further with our manager and subordinates' input. The rule was to do this process every 90 days and to have no more than three really important items you want to accomplish in that quarter. The most interesting aspect of this was that one-third of your bonus was determined by how your subordinates viewed your performance against the goals that were jointly developed.

As a member of the management team, we were required to go through our business processes as any customer would. As a novel concept, we also received our bill at home. They were somewhat incomprehensible—more so now with the vast array of taxes levied on wireless services. We spent time in customer care listening to customer calls and even taking some calls ourselves. (We did not install phones in our vehicles however: the technicians did.) To me this is part of the adage, "If you want to see how things really work, you must go to the factory floor." It works. It also gives you an appreciation for what the front-line employees experience daily. It gets you close to customers, too.

The recognition process is a terrific way to appreciate the way the culture was embedded in all employee daily activities. Each quarter, a meeting was held to determine who would be recognized as making a significant contribution to the business in the context of the goals and values. Co-workers submitted nominations. Management did not screen submissions. (There would be some screening by People Development ensuring no employee on a program would be recognized.) The selection process included the prior quarter's achievers (they were not called winners because there were no losers), line managers, and management. Awards were focused on the frontline employees; it was rare for managers of any stripe to be so recognized. The quarterly achievers were recognized at an all employee meeting that was great fun for everyone. It was a celebration of both team and individual success. As with all McCaw meetings, food was served. There was a high level of engagement with the mission of the company and each employee believed their voice and suggestions for improvement would be heard, considered, and acted upon.

District and regional achievers would form the nomination pool for the National Achievers Award. Those selected, using the same criteria and selection process, attended an awards event in Hawaii. At this event, achievers sat with senior management (including Craig McCaw) and aired further suggestions for improving the business, always in the context of our goals and values. These ideas were documented and were to be acted upon. My conclusion is that when employees are given a voice to improve the operation, it is seriously considered, and the best ideas are acted upon, employee morale and engagement soars. When People Development conducted Climate Surveys: the level of engagement with the job, the mission of the company, and being valued as a team member were continually in the high 90 percent range.

Rick Weston

ONE FINAL ANECDOTE, when I transferred to the headquarters office in Kirkland, WA, which was situated directly on the Yarrow Bay waterfront, the employees got the side with the view of the water and the Olympic range (though rarely visible in that lovely climate there) and my office, along with other managers, looked into the parking structure.

In time, there were a couple of disadvantages to the highly decentralized and independent organizational design, despite adherence to the goals and values. As a national company that outsourced its billing to a third party (and hence limited its product development capability) having 2,300 separate rate plans, tailored to each local market's whims, was unwieldy and expensive. There were some local branding inconsistencies due to this independence. The geographic-centric market structure made it difficult to rationalize National Account requirements. Finally, the reliance on local sales and distribution channels (i.e. dealers and other retailers) was expensive and was an impediment to developing a national brand due to inconsistent customer experiences. These issues needed to be resolved quickly as part of the acquisition of McCaw by AT&T. The cultural differences were profound as well. The brilliant culture developed by McCaw was subsumed by the AT&T tsunami. The new AT&T is a product of differing cultures resulting from the initial break-up and many subsequent mergers. The surviving, dominant entity of AT&T was Southwestern Bell. (I'll bet it was an interesting place to work.)

Qwest for Truth ...and Change

From an ethics perspective, which is the *raison d'être* for this book, it was imperfect at McCaw. The dealer network did have some integrity issues in the area of commissions. Some sales channels sought compensation for replacing an old cell number with a new one, which was hard for us to track initially. I had a situation where a sales person was terminated for "rolling numbers" (replacing old numbers with new ones, a phantom sale) but was later reinstated by Maggie after an appeal was made. This was a poor choice as it encouraged others to live dangerously. The McCaw model did permit, and somewhat encouraged, employees to take their grievances up the chain-of-command (this would never occur at AT&T). I had a salesperson call Craig McCaw on an issue that we disagreed on. There were no repercussions for that action.

I don't think such issues in the sales organization are uncommon. It was not pervasive. There were no attempts to "channel stuff" inventory. I don't ever recall there being initiatives to close the quarter, impair assets, meddle with reserves or any type of accounting irregularity. There was a great deal of focus in the early days on meeting the "debt covenants" as the company was funded with high-yield (junk) debt. I can offer no insight as to any machinations that may have been used to meet the covenants. It is also helpful to be part of a business that is growing like mad. Rapid growth is a blessing.

PERHAPS THE ABILITY to call the company founder on any issue would shine a bright light on anything untoward. Perhaps it is a function of goal Number One: Hire and develop great people

It was a great experience.

NINE

Qwest Communications International, Inc.

QWEST HAD THE ATTRIBUTES described in *Built to Last* where the entire rationale for the company was to bring about generational change in the communications industry. There was a fanatical belief at Qwest that we would change the world. Qwest represented the sea change from century old telephony to the Brave New World of Internet Protocol (IP) services. Qwest, led by Joe Nacchio, was going to disrupt the entire industry. This began initially from the fact the company would employ next-generation fiber optic technology—exclusively. This new market entrant would have a significantly lower cost structure while offering higher quality and greater reliability. This evolved momentously with the dawn of the Internet.

The Internet services revolution would enable Qwest to disrupt not only traditional telecommunications but also wide swaths of the

Qwest for Truth ...and Change

Qwest Headquarters after the US West merger.

Qwest's initial branding campaign logo

information technology category. In the years since it has become obvious: we use the Internet in all facets of our lives, all forms of services live in the cloud, and we have access to them anytime and anywhere. (At the time of this writing Amazon Web Services, Microsoft, and Google are the biggest beneficiaries and IBM, HP, and all PC makers are shrinking) The Internet in modern society is pervasive. It has been truly revolutionary. It was this fervent belief in the mission of Qwest that could have formed the building blocks of a great company that was indeed built to last. Alas, it was not to be.

It would seem the barriers to entry would be high with the capital investment required to build a new network, limiting the number of entrants. The incumbent providers (AT&T, MCI, Sprint, and many others) would be reluctant to cannibalize their existing service revenues as they had been waging a years-long market share and price war. It is counterintuitive today, but this was not the case then. Services such as broadband access (DSL) and web hosting initially generated incremental revenues. Capital poured into the industry. Innovative technology manufactured by new companies appeared daily, and startups were rewarded with eye-popping valuations. This created a reckless sense of urgency (or irrational exuberance).

The fact Qwest was a startup business provided it with the opportunity to create a corporate culture that could take advantage of its position in the market as a technically advantaged disruptor. Initially, the company was a construction business. As the network was being built, presentations were developed that laid out the claims of the coming revolution it would deliver. Corporate culture can be developed consciously or it can evolve. Despite Joe Nacchio's AT&T pedigree, or perhaps because of his reputation as a "break the mold" leader, the culture was an evolution rather than a planned approach similar to what McCaw nurtured. There was never a focus to articulate: "What type of company shall we become? What do we stand for? How do we expect our employees to act? What is the nature of our recognition and rewards system?" As Joe began to fill out his management team, no effort was made to think about culture. HR Executive Tom Matthews was brought in at the behest of the Anschutz group and was focused on HR processes, as well as keeping the troops in their swim lanes.

Qwest developed an early penchant for "spin." That is, spinning a yarn about what the company was doing and what it was going to become. Its revenues were initially derived solely from the construction business. Bringing in Joe represented a pivot away from being a wholesale carrier, once the construction was complete, to becoming a branded carrier designed to challenge AT&T. Our early efforts to market services were clumsy. We relied on Network Marketing companies to sell to consumers and small business. The order entry and billing systems barely functioned. The voice network had a minimal capacity, and we marketed a system that delivered a lot of busy signals. (QNC was used as the brand so as not to tarnish the Qwest brand) As the construction of the network progressed, Qwest was able to recognize revenues on a percent-completed basis but was also making dark fiber and IRU sales. These non-recurring revenues bolstered the view of huge revenue growth. This also marginalized barriers to market entry as fiber optic capacity was readily available. There was a buzz surrounding the company and its prospects. The presentations were making an impact and the company was positioned as very valuable and a great investment opportunity. Qwest went public on June 23, 1997, with great fanfare.

Stock option allocations to employees were an important element in attracting talent (as was being located in Denver). By this time, we had all heard of Microsoft administrative assistants becoming multi-millionaires from stock options. It was public information how many options were granted to Joe and his "16B" officers. The company was not very generous at granting stock options down the organization.

It was immediately obvious Qwest had a relentless focus on results. The work environment was chaotic, high energy, and fast paced. There was a not so subtle effort to exercise "courage and honor." This translated to sign up for the biggest commitment you can take on and courageously attack it. "Courage and honor" were used during the formulation of budgets to reach high on revenue goals and do yourself proud. It was an element of being challenged as to the worth of your contributions and indeed, your worth as a person. Understanding, as I did, that the intent of the company was to rapidly grow the business and seek to sell it, this imbued a strain of a mercenary culture. Senior management was focused on the kill; there was no tolerance for anything short of an all-out effort to win. Winning and being a winner was the theme. There was also an emphasis on "I," rather than "we." This was particularly true of Joe and his direct reports. Rarely used were the words "team" or "we". The targets were very high and there was a sense that doing whatever was required to get it done was expected.

As an example, when I was responsible for Product Management, my managers were expected to know the following about our competitors:

- Revenues
- Growth Rate
- Key Customers
- Principal contract terms
- Capital Expenditures
- Marketing Strategies
- Size of their sales force; their compensation plans
- Capital structure
- Market capitalization
- Operational centers and locations
- Key vendors
- Cost structure

Qwest for Truth ...and Change

When the PMs would present product plans, the "Stump the Stars" barrage would begin; most were not prepared for this. There is no question it would be valuable to know this information about one's competitors. We had no staff doing competitive analysis as AT&T did with armies to perform this function. We were trying to deliver stable products and were focused on pricing them appropriately to earn the returns contained in the business case. It was disheartening for the managers to work that hard and to always fall short of expectations.

There were no formal recognition programs at Qwest outside of the sales organizations. Keeping your job was recognition.

The organizational chaos was turbocharged with the string of acquisitions the company made. We called it evolution at web speed. We started small with Colorado Supernet that gave us access to a regional, dial-up Internet access network and customers. Later came ICON CMT that was a web design shop that catered to Big Pharma and others (winning a CLIO for the design of Nicole Miller's site, and designing the New York (football) Giants site). ICON also designed hardware and software solutions, hosting solutions, and served as the IT help desk for a number of large clients. Later came bigger acquisitions such as LCI International, which gave Qwest industrial strength billing and operations IT infrastructure. Ultimately, the big prize was the acquisition of US WEST.

Many strategic business relationships were formed as well. Developing these relationships, working on mergers and their integration were the vacation and weekend killers. I recall the development of a relationship with IBM to help Qwest design, build, and operate its Internet Data Centers. The deal was notable for culminating on St. Valentine's Day. Negotiations took place all day and stretched into the night with participants largely on the phone. It earned the name "The St. Valentine's Day Massacre" because Qwest was relentless at getting the deal consummated that night; no matter our partners had special events with their spouses or dates, which were utterly destroyed. As you would expect, that deal was not finalized that night, but we demonstrated courage and honor, or disrespect.

The merger with US West was a watershed event. It also represented a clash of cultures of the highest order. At the close of the merger, virtually all US West senior management left the firm. To the US West employees, whose culture more resembled AT&T's than Qwest's, the barbarians were inside the gate.

US West was a large, plodding, regulated monopoly although it did have a couple of units that were quite entrepreneurial. As with AT&T, their culture was steeped in history; tenure was valued, slow and steady carried the day. Like AT&T, revenues were barely staying level. The merger was to bring about synergies designed to spur growth and generate efficiencies. As with most mergers, layoffs are part of the plan. The out-of-the-gate number was 12,000 people would lose their jobs. US West revenue dwarfed those of Qwest—so did employee counts—and US West bore the brunt of the layoffs. (AT&T and US West were noted for giving employees lapel pins for service anniversaries, product launches, and sports sponsorships. Qwest managers joked they would receive 'synergy pins' when laid off) But to maintain momentum, revenue targets were stretched. Betsy Bernard, who was at AT&T when Joe was, had responsibility for the consumer segment. Ms. Bernard was told she needed to grow revenues by a double-digit percentage rate. This business had not grown in years and was actually forecast to shrink. Internet services were growing but were yet too small to make a big numerical impact. The wholesale unit had opportunities to contribute, but that became limited due to overcapacity in the fiber optic market and falling prices. Business sales had the opportunity to sell services nationally under the merger, and this could help growth, but it would take time.

Then, 9/11 hit, and that horrible day was followed by a recession.

I submit, market conditions coupled with a corporate culture that abhors failure led individuals to take actions to cover revenue gaps that were across the line. The subsequent litigation indicated:

- Contracts were backdated
- Side agreements were constructed and withheld from the financial community affecting revenue recognition
- Unauthorized discounts and contract terms were given
- Aggressive accounting was employed to accelerate revenue recognition

It seemed everything was for sale. I recall a discussion where it was suggested we sell our intellectual property. The target was US West's DSL database, arguably the best in the industry. It was shocking.

Did senior management instruct sales to make the numbers at any cost? No. That did not happen. I actually think Joe was horrified at the suggestion.

One misconception is that people broke the rules at Qwest because they were going to be personally rewarded regarding compensation or stock grants. This did not happen either. I believe bad behavior was driven by the culture where employees did not want to be perceived as failures and wanted to be part of the winning team. Many of the transactions deemed questionable by the regulatory authorities were not authored by sales, and no compensation was granted. At times, bonus pay was suspended for all managers. Stock options were not granted freely either. It wasn't about the money.

There is a component of American culture that is all about winning. The winning ethos at Qwest caused some to set aside their ethics (and what their mothers taught them) to help make the numbers and be a winner. Only once has the Super Bowl MVP come from a losing team (Super Bowl V, Chuck Howley, Dallas Cowboys). The confluence of the "I" culture and the need to be on a winning team represented the cultural defects exhibited at Qwest that resulted in its legal and regulatory issues, which nearly destroyed the company.

> **I got no friends 'cause they read the papers,**
>
> **they won't be seen with me ...**
>
> — Alice Cooper, *No More Mr. Nice Guy*

I received a call at my home from a number I did not recognize. The caller left a voice mail. It was Kris Hudson calling from the *Denver Post*. He was asking for any comments I might have regarding the litigation that was just released by the Securities and Exchange Commission (SEC) where I had been named in the civil litigation. (Wow.)

The night before, Kristine and I were discussing over dinner, the rumors circulating that the SEC and Justice Department were preparing to file complaints against Qwest and several of its employees. She asked if I was concerned about being included and I replied: "There is no chance. They're not interested in someone like me; they are interested in senior management, the decision makers."

While I was still employed at Qwest, our general counsel, Drake Tempest (great name for a Yale-educated lawyer) distributed a memo indicating we were under a "document hold," and all emails, other correspondence, and work products were to be retained. To my knowledge, this edict was followed faithfully. I was asked to attend a number of meetings with various other employees and lawyers and review any number of documents. There was a room I was escorted through where some 30 to 40 consultants were going through all the documents they could find on the system and the entire e-mail archive. They had been printing documents and putting them in boxes. You could have filled a railcar with all of the boxes of documents.

I was invited to a meeting where I faced three separate law firms with about a dozen lawyers total. They were all interested in different aspects of what transpired at Qwest. I answered all of their questions, to the best of my knowledge, over several hours.

Additionally, the FBI interviewed me. They were interested in similar events, but their probe was more specific, attempting to learn how certain individuals had benefitted financially by certain transactions. In particular, they wanted to know how it was that Qwest executives were granted shares in a wide variety of companies with whom Qwest did business. The FBI produced a spreadsheet that contained the names of a number of senior executives, a listing of companies, and the dollar amounts of stock transactions attributable to each. Two things were at play with this: First, any number of investment bankers wanted to do business with Qwest. As they brought out new companies via IPOs, Qwest executives were granted

"Friends and Family" shares. Additionally, on many occasions we were asked to include new vendors in our product plans. These companies were pre-IPO, and Qwest was able to purchase warrants in the firm. As well, executives were granted shares in the firm. As the company neared its IPO debut, Qwest would put out a press release that indicated we were using their products, which helped boost the stock's value. These activities increased the complexity of our network by adding new vendors. Each had to be integrated into the operational, order entry, and billing systems. It served to further enrich the executives. It would have been nice to have these shares spread to the teams working on integrating this new technology, but it did not happen and was against the "I" culture. I did receive shares twice and made some money, about $20,000. When this activity was exposed, Phil Anschutz determined it didn't look great and decided to donate his proceeds totaling $4.4 million to charity. This meeting was not tense and I cooperated fully and answered all of the agents' questions even elaborating beyond the direct question itself. I asked them why they wore their side arms in the office? I was told it was policy, but knew it was an intimidation tactic to underscore how serious they were and how important this Qwest mess was. It didn't bother me; I wasn't intimidated. I had nothing to hide. One agent told me they even wore their side arms on airplanes during personal travel as instructed by their chain-of-command. It was just after 9/11 after all.

On October 9 and 10 of 2002, I testified in a deposition at the SEC that, oddly enough, was located on the 15th floor of the Qwest Tower: our headquarters building in Denver. The law firm Boies, Shiller and Flexner, was representing me. This firm also represented Qwest Corporation. My attorneys were David Boyd and Tim Rossman who made clear that Qwest's interests were superior to my own and that their representation of me would reflect that fact in the event a conflict arose. (*Well, isn't that special?* I thought) I was presented with a copy of the subpoena the SEC had sent to counsel that included a cover letter signed by Kirsten Gillibrand. At that time, she was with Boies, Shiller and Flexner, now the junior Senator from New York who replaced Hillary Clinton.

My strategy in this deposition was to be forthcoming, tell the truth, and explain what happened at Qwest. On the first day, I met with Meredith Munro (no relation to the Colonel Munro in *The Last of the Mohicans* who had his heart cut out by Magua on the battlefield). Also attending was Susie Youn, the SEC Branch Chief. Ms. Munro wanted to discuss a variety of transactions I had been directly involved in. Their interest was the transactions between Qwest and KMC Telecom that were valued at several hundred million dollars collectively. Naturally, they had all of the relevant documents and e-mails. I went way beyond the basic answers many of my colleagues such as, "yes," or, "no." I never gave the favorite answer used by others: "I don't recall." During the question and answer sessions, I would go to the easel and draw pictures of how things worked in telephony and the Internet as well as educating them on product "S" curves, break even points, and other elements that provided both context and granularity. My deposition lasted from 9:20 a.m. to 4:30 p.m. with a break for lunch.

On October 10, 2002, we began the deposition at 8:30 a.m. with all of the previous players plus the addition of Maria Sepulveda from the SEC. The predominant discussion was a continuation of the KMC relationship, the structure of the agreements, and the goals of the projects. I could have easily provided them with the same justification that Mr. Wilks did: these projects represented Qwest's ability to expand its services using a different capital structure for a technology that was going to become obsolete shortly. This strategy was true at the outset but had grown to encompass delivering revenue against shortfalls. Thus, I also provided them with the understanding of the "revenue gap closing" initiatives. (You know, the real truth.)

Toward the end of the day, well after 3 p.m., the discussion shifted to the transaction with Genuity. At the conclusion of the KMC testimony, Ms. Munro indicated to her associates that it went well, and I was "very forthcoming." Maria Sepulveda was the SEC examiner for this particular transaction, although she seemed unfamiliar with the material and directionless in her questioning. Susie Youn was coaching her through some of the documents and prodding her to go in a particular direction with her questions. I recall at one point after a rambling dissertation asking, "Is there a question here"? Hours were spent understanding and documenting the KMC transactions. Minutes were spent on the Genuity transaction.

On February 13, 2013 Ms. Youn traveled to Seattle to interview the Regional Vice-president for sales with responsibility for the Genuity account. Her name is Susan Ershler. Ms. Sepulveda joined by telephone. Her deposition began at 9:10 a.m., and was finished at 2:38 p.m. Several breaks in the testimony were noted in the record. In her role, Ms. Ershler was the principal negotiator for the Genuity agreement and was deeply involved in the development of the contract terms. In her deposition, Ms. Ershler indicates the meeting with Genuity on September 13, 2000 was the first time she ever heard of the structure of the transaction as two separate agreements (Pages 39 and 48). This discussion was in response to the question of what I wrote on the whiteboard during this meeting. Ms. Ershler's testimony conflicts with the presentation that was given to her manager dated August 15, 2000 that, on page 2, it expressly states the concept of two contracts and an equipment sale. Ms. Ershler further stated that she stayed in Boston for a week to finalize the terms of the agreement. Ms. Youn agreed with Ms. Ershler's attorney that she was very cooperative (and the mints served were "strong").

On February 23, 2002, a midday press conference aired on national television. Attorney General John Ashcroft and SEC Chairman William Donaldson were the hosts. All totaled, there were four individuals named by Mr. Ashcroft in a criminal case and eight individuals named by Mr. Donaldson in the SEC civil litigation. (The criminal defendants were also named in companion civil litigation). It was in this forum the litigation against me was announced. This effort was part of President George W. Bush's crackdown on white-collar crime. It came a mere 10 days after Ms. Ershler's deposition.

Throughout the day, I received calls from the *Wall Street Journal*, *New York Times,* and other media outlets asking for comments. I even had a reporter from the *Rocky Mountain News* come to my house to ask for comments. It was snowing outside.

Typically in civil actions by the SEC, one is issued a "Wells Notice." The Wells Notice stemmed from a 1972 committee. It is named after John Wells and the committee he served on in 1972 to review and evaluate the SEC's enforcement policies and practices. The "Wells Notice" stemmed from that committee's recommendations. A "Wells Notice" is a letter sent by the regulator to inform you they are considering litigation and it is to include the substance of the allegations. It provides that person an opportunity to indicate why the litigation would not be appropriate and may forestall the filing of said complaint by submitting his argument in writing to the decision makers at the SEC.

With Bush administration's need to show it was serious about business scofflaws, and the hasty decision by the SEC to hold a press conference, I was not afforded a "Wells Notice."

I view this as an ambush because I was caught in the political maw. My attorney told me to, "Get over it," because a Wells Notice is not required by law. I am clearly not, "Over it."

I accessed the complaint against me, and the others, on the SEC web site. I didn't understand the allegations completely (such as violating Section 17(a) of the Securities Act of 1933). I did understand the implication of paragraph 13 where "each defendant was to disgorge all ill-gotten gains from their participation in the fraud including all benefits derived from their employment at Qwest such as salary, bonuses, stock, and other remuneration, and prejudgment and post-judgment interest thereon." So, they are asking for every dime I ever made at Qwest plus interest? Harsh. Terrifying.

Immediately after the complaint by the SEC was issued, the criminal prosecutors asked for and received, a stay. From the Davidoff Law Firm:

Note:
There is a difference in the scope of criminal and civil discovery. In a civil proceeding, anything relevant to the case that is not privileged is discoverable. In contrast, discovery under the Federal Rules of Criminal Procedure is highly restricted, reflecting the Fifth Amendment right not to incriminate oneself and the Sixth Amendment right to confront witnesses. The contrast is illustrated by the differences in the civil and criminal deposition process. Under the civil rules, parties may depose all parties to the action and any other person necessary to obtain testimony relevant to the subject matter. Under the Criminal rules, however, only depositions of a party's own witnesses may be taken, and then only pursuant to a court order.

Qwest for Truth ...and Change

Essentially, the stay was granted in support of the Constitutional rights of the criminal defendants. For me and the other civil litigants, the case was frozen. This meant the allegations stood as they were written, and those interested parties (including family members) read the words while I was unable to refute them or defend myself in any way.

As I sat in Denver stewing, I thought: *I was a cooperating witness. I didn't falsify anything. The accountants signed off on all these deals. I didn't make any representations to stock or bondholders. I didn't receive a Wells Notice. I was implicated on national TV. My picture appeared in the newspapers along with the allegations. The government wants all my money. My consulting work dried up. I am unemployable in Corporate America. I thought the SEC would value my honesty and willingness to be "forthcoming" and would be interested in litigating the decision-makers rather than me.* Later, I would learn one of the principal measurements of effectiveness at the SEC is the "number of enforcement actions." Scalps. This was not good…At all.

Luckily, I was able to secure other consulting work to make ends meet. A former Qwest colleague was named the CEO of a software company based in Israel, working on virtualization. I assisted in their product's development and contract negotiations. I learned a great deal about the Middle East and frankly was terrified on my first couple of visits to Tel Aviv. (The Israelis sure do a thorough job of airport screening.]

The litigation continued. The reality is that most people believe the adage, "Where there is smoke there is fire," rather than innocent until proven guilty (or liable in this case) I offer you some text from a letter I received. The letter emanated from the General Services Administration for the Federal government. It suspended me from, "participation in any Federal procurement and non-procurement (sic) programs." Section 4 of the letter read: "The civil complaint filed against you by the Government in the United States District Court for the District of Colorado constitutes adequate evidence that you committed the acts charged and provides a cause for your suspension pursuant to FAR 9.407-2(a)(3) and (5) and 9.407-2(c)." *The complaint constitutes adequate evidence you committed the acts* are the words of my government which guarantees my rights. Well.

As time inched along, glacially, I sought legal representation distinct from Qwest's attorneys at Boies, Schiller and Flexner. By this time, others had retained all of the attorneys in Denver with experience in these matters. Qwest's general counsel, Rich Baer, and I met to finalize an indemnification agreement. This Agreement, Affirmation and Undertaking for the Advancement of Expenses, provides: that I acted in good faith and that my conduct in an official capacity was in the company's best interests, or at least not opposed to the company's best interests, and that I have no reasonable cause to believe my conduct was unlawful, among other provisions. The agreement served to pay my legal fees during this ordeal. Coincident with that agreement was a joint defense agreement with Qwest's principal counsel Wilmer, Cutler and Pickering. This was a pretty one-sided agreement where Qwest maintained its attorney-client privilege, but Qwest could unilaterally decide to disclose any information provided by me to any third party. This was done in the context of Qwest cooperating with regulatory, congressional, DOJ investigations, as well as private litigants. Having completed these items, I was introduced to Doug Lobel from Morgan, Lewis and Bockius (MLB) based in Washington D.C. While I was staying at the Grand Wailea resort in Maui, Mr. Lobel sent to me the terms of the representation. I was asked to sign a consent and waiver document acknowledging that MLB represented Qwest's interests in other matters.

Contained in the waiver was the following:

> Similarly, while we will not represent Mr. Weston in claims or litigation directly adverse to Qwest (indeed, we would withdraw our representation of Mr. Weston under those circumstances), or in any matter arising from Qwest's indemnification of Mr. Weston, we have discussed the possibility that Mr. Weston may testify or act in a way contrary to Qwest's interests.

In shorthand, I did what I was asked to do: structure transactions to further Qwest's goals. I followed the rules and had accounting representatives present during the negotiations. I followed their advice. On the filing of the litigation, the SEC wanted all my money. My legal representation was paid for by Qwest, but under terms that could have turned adverse. I would estimate that my legal fees for this matter were greater than $350,000. (Remember, Joe Nacchio's legal expenses were on the order of $75 million) I could never have afforded to provide my own legal representation. Thus, signing these agreements was never in doubt.

I was angry. Actually, I'm still angry. I told my attorney I wanted to fight the charges, go to trial, to take my chances. Mr. Lobel must have told me 100 times…no: "A jury trial in Denver? The people of Denver hate Qwest…. The press coverage has been brutal…. You can never predict what a jury will do…. These cases never go to trial; everyone settles…. The penalties for liability are much higher than if you settle…. I cannot recommend in good conscience that you go to trial. I am recommending that you settle this case with the SEC."

In civil litigation, the standard is lower than in criminal cases. In a criminal case, the standard of proof is: "Beyond a reasonable doubt." The jury must decide the case unanimously. In civil litigation, the standard for liability is much lower: "Does the preponderance of the evidence presented make it more likely than not the person is liable?" A civil jury requires a simple majority. You may recall that O.J. Simpson was acquitted of criminal murder charges but found liable in his civil case filed by the Brown and Goldman families. This is an example of the difference. In a civil action, there is no right to a speedy trial. The Sword of Damocles hung over my head for 2,325 days. It was not until July 8, 2008 that I reached a settlement agreement with the SEC.

Settlement discussions with the SEC had several fits and starts. My attorney left MLB for Arnold and Porter and discussions took place in January 2006. Mr. Lobel left for Cooley, Godward, Kronish, and settlement discussions took place in August of 2008.

On August 12, 2008, I was granted a settlement conference with magistrate judge Michael E. Hegarty. At the SEC, the investigators who prepare the case and file the litigation are different from those who proceed to trial or settlement conferences. I met the two SEC lawyers at the Byron G. Rogers United States Courthouse. My attorney tried to introduce me to them, but I refused to shake their hands or say much (still mad). The process provides that the SEC lawyers meet with the magistrate judge separate from the defendant. This was it. When I got my chance to tell my side of the story, I told that magistrate judge how the government had it all wrong. I was overcome with tears. I cried very hard as all of my personal anguish, anger, and trauma came rushing out of me. I did get to make my case, in private, with the matter realistically settled.

After I stopped crying, I did not decide to write this book; that came later.

We reached a settlement on July 9, 2009 with the SEC. The SEC announced on July 23, 2009 it had reached settlements with Joel Arnold, Grant Graham, and Richard Weston. This is a passage from that statement posted on the SEC website: *Also, without admitting or denying the allegations in the Commission's complaint, Weston consented to the entry of a judgment enjoining him from violating Section 13(b)(5) of the Exchange Act and Rule 13b2-1 thereunder, and from aiding and abetting violations of Sections 13(a) and 13 (b)(2) of the Exchange Act and Rules 12b-20, 13a-1 and 13a-13 thereunder. The judgment also requires Weston to pay a civil penalty of $20,000.*

Mr. Lobel characterized the entry of judgment as: "You have the same obligation as the rest of us; not to break the law."

I was required to submit a cashier's check to the SEC no later than July 22, 2009 in the amount of $20,000. I received confirmation that the check had been received and was, in fact, signed for by "Pete." On July 9, 2010, I received a five-page letter from the SEC that indicated they had no record of my payment and articulated the various and sundry means available to them to collect the unpaid levy. (*Really?*) I was able to acquire a copy of the check from my bank, replete with stamp of both the U.S. Treasury and the SEC, indicating it had been successfully negotiated. Simultaneously, I received an e-mail from my attorney that included a letter from the SEC indicating, in essence: *Just kidding, we got the money. Have a nice day!*

TEN

and change...

IN THE BROADEST TERMS, have we solved the problems that led to what transpired at Qwest? What about the events at Enron and MCI WorldCom? Are the stock options issuance and backdating issues forever solved? What about the effectiveness of Sarbanes-Oxley designed to solve the issues raised by the preceding? Do we have durable solutions for effective corporate governance? What about the SEC? Is the SEC effective in preventing these events? These issues will be explored in this chapter.

Consider a different deal: An investment banker is asked by management to develop a relationship with a widely respected Fortune 10 company. This firm is very active in mergers and acquisitions, but his company is not participating. The individual gets involved in a project where the investment bank is asked to purchase some of the company's assets. The deal is structured where the company will repurchase the assets at a later date and the bank will make a small profit. There is virtually no risk in the deal for the bank. Success in the deal will mean future business for the investment bank. This transaction is the Nigerian electricity-producing barge deal. The players were Enron and Merrill Lynch. The investment banker is Daniel Bayly who was sentenced to 30 months in prison for fraud. Mr. Bayly was the head of investment banking at Merrill Lynch. He had a stellar 30-year career at Merrill. His life turned on a five-minute phone call with Andy Fastow of Enron. The deal was a fraud because the risk of loss did not pass to Merrill Lynch. Mr. Bayly received no compensation from the deal, and he did not sign any of the contracts.

Enron

The Enron case is an examination of their corporate culture. Enron's board of directors suspended its code-of-conduct when it allowed Andy Fastow to create off-balance sheet entities designed to mask debt and manufacture revenue while allowing Mr. Fastow to personally profit. These special purpose entities were but one of a number of measures Enron took to manage its earnings. At one point, 13% of outstanding stock were options held by management, many with a three-year vesting schedule. Obviously, Enron was engaged in financial engineering to the benefit of pumping up its share price. $70 billion of market value was wiped out and many longtime employees were left with nothing. Previously, Enron was named, by *Fortune Magazine*, as "America's Most Innovative Company…" for six years in a row.

Arthur Andersen

Another casualty of the Enron scandal was Arthur Andersen (AA), one of the most reputable auditors in the country. AA was accused of helping Enron structure deals and managing the accounting process to facilitate revenue recognition. AA was accused of destroying documents relevant to the investigation of the business practices of Enron. It was believed that AA took this risk on to enable its consulting arm to benefit from the relationship. In 2000, AA earned $25 million from Enron in audit fees and another $27 million in consulting fees. AA was criminally convicted of obstruction of justice and was forced to surrender its CPA licenses, which put the firm out of business. The consulting business had been split off and now operates as Accenture. The Supreme Court eventually overturned the AA conviction, but the entity no longer existed. Talk about a hollow victory.

MCI WorldCom

The case of MCI WorldCom is a matter where the firm masked its financial performance by treating operating expenses (in this case access charges paid to telephone companies for completing calls) as capital investments. Access charges were one of the single largest operating expenses long distance companies had. This subterfuge lowered operating expenses, which affected the income statement; and the costs placed on the balance sheet were then depreciated over time. At the time, most in the industry could not understand how MCI WorldCom could price its services so aggressively and remain profitable. The amount of the fraud was $3.8 billion and was uncovered by an internal accounting department. It was subsequently discovered the fraud totaled $11 billion. When the company collapsed, $180 billion in market value was wiped out along with 30,000 jobs. The CEO, Bernard Ebbers was sentenced to 25 years in prison. Mr. Ebbers borrowed prodigiously from

Qwest for Truth ...and Change

Bank of America using his MCI WorldCom stock as collateral. The loan total ballooned to $400 million at the time of the collapse of the firm, and MCI WorldCom eventually assumed the balance, relieving Bank of America of the loan. In a very unusual twist, ten members of the Board of Directors agreed to personally contribute $18 million as part of a $54 million settlement. Typically, members of a company's board are indemnified from liability, and directors' and officers' insurance covers any financial sanctions.

Adelphia Communications Corporation

Adelphia Communications was a cable TV operator based in Coudersport, PA. The company founder, John Rigas, his son Timothy, and other insiders were charged with masking $2.3 billion in liabilities by placing them in off-balance sheet entities similar to Enron. They also were charged with providing falsified operating statistics to the investment community as well as self-dealing; (using company funds for personal expenses to buy real estate). Mr. Rigas was convicted and sentenced to 15 years in prison, and Timothy was sentenced to 25 years in prison after his conviction. Time Warner Cable and Comcast acquired the company's assets while it was in bankruptcy. Different than most cases, the Rigas' did not perpetrate a fraud to sell their stock; they used the company as if it were privately held, and used its cash to fund a lavish lifestyle. Perhaps Mr. Rigas felt he was entitled as the founder.

TYCO

Tyco is a conglomerate with a diverse set of business put together by its former CEO, Dennis Kozlowski. Mr. Kozlowski was widely viewed as a brilliant executive as he built this firm through mergers and acquisitions. Mr. Kozlowski and CFO Mark Swartz were charged with a scheme to personally enrich themselves through stock options; loans made by the company that were subsequently forgiven; using corporate funds for personal expense; and unauthorized bonus payments. The case was uncovered when Mr. Kozlowski was attempting to thwart the New York tax authorities of one million dollars by indicating the purchase of art was for Tyco's headquarters (located in Bermuda) rather than Mr. Kozlowski's New York apartment. The New York apartment was also highlighted for surreal excesses of lavish spending, including $15,000 for a dog-shaped umbrella stand, $6,000 for a shower curtain, and $2,200 for a gold-plated trash can. Both Kozlowski and Swartz were sentenced up to 25 years in prison; they were to pay a combined $134 million in restitution; Mr. Kozlowski was fined $70 million, and Mr. Swartz was fined $35 million. Mr. Kozlowski was recently released, having served nearly seven years in prison. Mr. Swartz was released from prison after serving eight years. The Tyco case is different from the others in that the company did not go through bankruptcy. In fact, Tyco is a thriving business with a market capitalization over $18 billion.

Qwest

The allegations at Qwest were principally related to the recognition of revenues (at the point of sale rather than over the term of the agreement), the noneconomic nature of certain transactions that should not be considered revenue totaling $3.1 billion, and the exclusion of $71.3 million in expenses. Qwest settled the litigation by restating $2.2 billion in revenues. The criminal conviction of Joe

Qwest for Truth ...and Change

Nacchio was based on charges of insider trading. Joe was acquitted on 23 counts and convicted on 19 counts. He was ordered to pay a $19 million fine and forfeit $52 million of stock sale gains. Joe was sentenced to six years in prison and was released after serving four years. There was no parole term. At the conclusion of Joe's trial, Judge Edward Nottingham said: "The crimes the defendant has been found guilty of are crimes of overarching greed."

So much for Gordon Gekko's "Greed is good" articulation so widely quoted.

There are several threads common to all of the actors listed above. From any perspective, all of them were wealthy and would have lived very comfortable lives had their scandals not taken place. They were driven in some measure by greed. This not to say greed in all cases is bad. All entrepreneurs may, at some point, be characterized as greedy. "Greed" may arise to protect their intellectual property, to capture market share, to eliminate their competition, to seek rents from government, among other examples. Entrepreneurs, artists, musicians, authors, and actors all seek to benefit financially from their work and protect it from illicit copies. Greed among these businessmen (yes, all the examples above involved men only) was extreme and hard to understand.

Additionally, all of these men went to jail, and many lost all of their wealth. Recently, much has been made about the fact that no individuals were jailed for their role in the housing market meltdown. Bernie Ebbers and John Rigas essentially received life sentences due to their age. Enron's Jeffrey Skilling was sentenced to 25 years as was Dennis Kozlowski of Tyco. Only in the USA are the sentences for these types of crimes this long. In contrast, the average sentence for homicide is 18 years and for sex crimes, the average is 7.1 years. The punishment for white-collar crime is very harsh. Some argue tough sentencing laws serve as a deterrent. The current political movement to decriminalize victimless crimes such as drug offenses is a stark contrast to this notion.

As stated earlier, I think Joe Nacchio was not motivated by money for himself. I think his motivation was to demonstrate AT&T made a mistake not elevating him to CEO and he was determined to damage them.

The Adelphia case suggests John Rigas believed the company was his to use as he wished since he was the founder, irrespective of the fact it became a public company, which made him accountable to its shareowners.

> **"*Man has the power to act as his own destroyer —and that is the way he has acted through most of his history.*"**
>
> —Ayn Rand

No one should come away with the perception that criminal greed is rampant in our system of capitalism. Of the thousands of public companies, only a tiny fraction has suffered the fate of these companies. Our system of capitalism has lifted more people from poverty than any other. Our system of Madison's governmental design, coupled with capitalism, has made America into the greatest nation on Earth. These scandals are the failure of *man* not the failure of our system. In fact, given the rarity of these events, our system works remarkably well, and our corporate leaders are genuinely good and decent people. Many scions of American business have pledged their fortunes to charity. Many have made significant contributions to institutions of higher learning and medicine.

In further defense of capitalism, I note that in the recent Democrat primary election Sen. Bernie Sanders made his central theme around: "The Wall Street's business model is fraud." Wall Street has bad actors to be sure. In the main, Wall Street provides the ability for good ideas and business models to come to fruition through our capital markets. Sen. Sanders is a champion of putting people to work through public infrastructure projects. Wall Street has been providing funding for infrastructure projects through the issuance of municipal bonds for decades. These financing vehicles make possible: water treatment, roads and bridges, dormitories, airports, tunnels, power plants, bike paths, and any number of infrastructure projects to the benefit of our citizens. Our capital markets are part of the reason why our living standards are so high. It is misguided to suggest that our banking system and Wall Street are solely to blame for our economic situation.

In a prior chapter, I wrote at length about corporate culture. Every organization has some sort of culture coursing through it. It is a reflection of how management values its employees; how it perceives itself in the markets in which it participates; and how it expects to act in carrying out its activities. It may be formalized and visible as in the case of McCaw Cellular. Or it may be personified by the indoctrination of new employees by the "Elders" as in the case of AT&T. In the above examples, an existing corporate culture may have been inherited from a prior management team and Chief Executive. Some elements of the corporate culture may have survived and even been further developed and ingrained. At Qwest, there was no interest in establishing a corporate culture built around a set of values as was the case at McCaw Cellular. In any event, these executives must have believed any rules or norms embedded in the culture of their firm did not apply to them. In the case of Enron, the Board of Directors suspended the Code of Conduct, enabling personal enrichment. Tyco executives abused bonus programs for themselves, and a key employee loan program, by self-indulging in loan forgiveness. No sustainable corporate culture would have contemplated such favorable treatment for executives. Bernie Ebbers was highly leveraged using his stock as collateral for $400 million in loans and was personally invested in artificially inflating the stock value of MCI Worldcom. Clearly, none of their activities would have been permissible under any corporate culture rooted in ethical behavior. Businesses showcased in *Built to Last* all had a corporate culture oriented around a calling to a monumental organization where the goals of the firm supersede the financial ambitions of certain executives, including founders. In the end, the executives mentioned above placed their narrow, personal interests over the firm, its employees, and its shareowners. You will never find that in the culture of America's greatest firms. Fortunately, it is a rare occurrence in business, although it receives the loudest attention.

In response to these scandals was the implementation of new laws and regulations under the aegis of Sarbanes-Oxley (SOX). Paul Sarbanes (D-MD) and Michael Oxley (R-OH) authored this law. This legislation was far-reaching and covered many areas. It increased oversight through the Public Company Accountability and Oversight Board to monitor the activities of auditors. It also increased SEC resources and enhanced their ability to implement penalties. The law also addressed conflicts of interests in the stock analyst community and with auditors and consultants, (specifically aimed at Arthur Andersen and Andersen Consulting). The law increased the penalties for white-collar crimes and increased the accountability of corporate officers. There was a section that required enhanced financial disclosures, targeting off-balance sheet disclosures among many others. The most contentious aspect of SOX is Section 404, which requires management and the external auditor to report on the adequacy of the company's internal controls with the regard to financial reporting. This is the most costly aspect of the legislation for companies to implement, as documenting and testing important financial manual and automated controls require enormous effort.

Under Section 404 of the Act, management is required to produce an "internal control report" as part of each annual Exchange Act report. The report must affirm "the responsibility of management for establishing and maintaining an adequate internal control structure and procedures for financial reporting." The report must also "contain an assessment, as of the end of the most recent fiscal year of the firm, of the effectiveness of the internal control structure and procedures of the issuer for financial reporting." The initial concern for this portion was related to the cost of compliance. The law has since been modified to lower the burden for smaller firms. There is a group of lawmakers who believe one effect of the law has been to stifle the IPO market as new firms must meet these regulatory burdens, demonstrating expansive controls. There are provisions to "claw back" from company executive's pecuniary gains from illicit transactions. SOX has been praised for nurturing an ethical culture as it forces top management to be transparent and employees to be responsible for their acts while protecting whistleblowers.

Stated plainly, the CEO and CFO of a public company are to sign off on the accuracy of their financial reports and the adequacy of its financial controls or face stiff criminal penalties. Thus, John Flannery, the new CEO of GE, must certify across a global conglomerate with over 20 business units and hundreds of thousands of employees and transactions that every aspect of its accounting is pristine. I'm not sure that level of assurance is possible, but GE is a great company with a renowned corporate culture. Recently, I have noted a concern being aired that many companies are providing pro-forma or "adjusted" earnings releases as part of their "headline" quarterly disclosure, also characterized as non-GAAP. (As an example, LinkedIn reported "adjusted" earnings of $950 million, but under GAAP it lost $240 million, according to WSJ, 6-21-2016) It is still the case that many important accounting activities are described in footnotes that may not be well understood by some investors. With the infinitesimally small number of public-company accounting scandals over the last decade, one could argue the law has been effective. Alternatively, one could argue the law is an unnecessary overreach as the incidence of corporate fraud is rare.

One of the elements of the law includes the protection of whistleblowers. The action is handled by the Department of Labor. Initially, the law was poorly constructed as it applied only to the publicly traded entity thus did not pertain to whistleblowers in subsidiaries. Further court cases included the action to apply it to contractors and subcontractors. Prior to this, from 2002 to 2008, there were 1,273 complaints, but only 17 were ruled in favor of the whistleblower. One of the outcomes of a successful whistleblower case includes back pay and benefits, reinstatement (yikes) and special damages resulting from the ordeal. Among the concerns about this provision is it would create new causes of action where none existed before, inducing a number of law firms to vigorously pursue these actions by. These actions are time-consuming and expensive to pursue as the employee may be caught in the maw for years. Additionally, some argue the law can be used in an overreaching fashion. This was exemplified in a case where a Florida fisherman was charged under Sarbanes-Oxley for destroying evidence when he tossed undersized red grouper back in the water. The late (great) Antonin Scalia opined during the oral arguments at the Supreme Court, "He could have gotten 20 years! What kind of a sensible prosecution is that?" There is a thread in business today that the government is smothering businesses with far-reaching regulations and using them in novel and corrosive ways. The laws of good intentions are also filled with unintended consequences. This is particularly troubling when anti-business sentiment is increasing.

In that vein, there was a follow-on legal development known as the Thompson Memorandum. It was issued in 2003 by then Deputy Attorney General Larry Thompson. It was designed to provide guidance within the DOJ for determining whether to charge a corporation with a crime when misconduct is suspected. There are a number of factors to be considered including:

- The nature and seriousness of the offense
- The risk of harm to the public
- The pervasiveness of wrongdoing at the company
- A history at the company of wrongdoing
- The level of cooperation and production of documents at the firm

- The existence and adequacy of the firm's compliance programs
- The firm's remedial action
- Collateral consequences to shareholders, pensioners, and employees

The controversial provisions of the Thompson Memorandum dealt with the Constitutional rights of the defendants:

- Should the firm indemnify the employee and cover their legal fees?
- Can the firm be allowed to waive the attorney-client and work-product privileges regarding facts uncovered through an internal investigation?

The firestorm arose when the presiding view was the "corporation" was fully cooperating with the government only if it *did not pay* attorney's fees for employees and *agreed to waive* the attorney-client and work-product privilege. As was the case for Arthur Andersen, a criminal indictment is a death sentence for a company. Thus, the firm's impulse is for self-survival even if your rights of due process are subjugated. This legal strategy was highly criticized in a case involving several KPMG employees who worked on tax shelters. It has since been revised (by the McNulty Memo) to strike down the notion that company cooperation must deny employees the advancement of their legal fees. The memo also modifies the subsuming of attorney-client privilege by requiring prosecutors receive written authorization from the U.S. Deputy Attorney General. Unfortunately, this law enables prosecutors waging war on white-collar crime to pit firms against its employees. While helping prosecutors, this law may discourage more ethical employee behaviors at work. As

Georgetown University professor John Hasnas put it: "Despite what DOJ may think, there is more to ethics than helping its prosecutors collect scalps." (WSJ 03-11-2006)

What should companies do?

- Companies should have policies that provide an Ombudsman for employees. This entails having a direct line to a member of the Board of Directors or a member of the senior management team. This requires a commitment to a policy of open communication. This is a difficult step to take because of the potential time commitment or restraints of a board member. It also requires the education of the workforce as to what kinds of behaviors rise to the level of the Ombudsman and what kind of response they will receive. The Board of Directors has to be seriously committed to making this work. Otherwise, the employees will see it as a mockery and it will have a negative effect on morale.

- Devote adequate energy and resources to research the concerns raised by the employee and ensure follow through. This may require that the board's Ombudsman work through a functional group, in most cases, Human Resources (or People Development).

- The firm should engage in the extensive use of climate surveys and other anonymous communications vehicles. The results of the climate surveys should be important enough to become part of the goal setting and MBO process in the line organizations. Employee satisfaction efforts cannot be delegated to the HR department.

- The firm must commit to constant communications about its Code of Conduct (or Ethics) and publicly reward exemplary actions. Inappropriate actions must be identified and called out. This does not mean public humiliation of the employee, only their actions. A management environment of improvement through coaching and development plans for the employee is appropriate, as is termination for repeat offenders.

- The firm must have a focus on continuous improvement that removes loopholes, as well as opportunities for working in the gray space. The processes' goal reinforces the integrity of the business practice and the individuals performing these functions. The initiative requires a managerial skill to balance conformity with innovation. Naturally, management skill development is paramount to achieve this balance.

- A programmatic approach to elevate the roles of the firm's goals and values and the importance of ethical behavior is required. Recognition programs and promotional opportunities should be the visible manifestation of embracing and living the corporate culture.

- The consequences for failing to adhere to the corporate culture and value system should be well understood. These processes have universal applicability in the areas of diversity, governance, and harassment issues as well. They are all interconnected and make up the fabric of the culture. Employees who know what is expected of them and where the bright lines of acceptable behaviors reside will be more engaged and productive.

Qwest for Truth ...and Change

What should prospective employees look for?

- Seek companies that are serious about creating an inclusive culture that values open, upward communications.
- Evaluate the treatment of those using the process and their ability to effect change.
- Gauge management's reaction to issues brought before them.
- Evaluate how the firm's management adheres to their corporate culture and goals and values. Do they walk the walk?
- If you are uncomfortable: leave. You do not want to be caught in the maw of the whistleblower process or subject to the provisions of the Thompson Memorandum.

What about our Regulations and Laws?

In 2001, there was an issue at Apple Computer (as it was called then) regarding the backdating of stock options. Steve Jobs, who was accepting a salary of $1 per year, was awarded $ 7.5 million in options. The options were awarded a strike price of $21.01 on December 18, 2001. The company back-dated the options to October 19, 2001 at a price of $18.30. This provided Steve Jobs with a paper gain of $20 million that must be recorded as an expense on Apple's books. The problem is by not taking the $20 million expense, Apple's performance was exaggerated. In his deposition, Steve Jobs indicated he "...did not have an appreciation of the accounting implications." What are we going to do, indict the most innovative American for options backdating? Not being aware of the "accounting implications" would not be an appropriate defense under Sarbanes-Oxley; zealous prosecutors could have pursued criminal charges.

Warren Buffett, Chairman of Berkshire Hathaway and prescient investor, was a proponent of changing the regulations regarding the accounting treatment of stock options. He argued stock options were used as compensation but were disclosed as footnotes rather than on the income statement and this distorted the profitability of companies using them. (This is also prevalent today in the release of "adjusted earnings") This allowed some companies to pay lower cash compensation, artificially inflating their profitability, he argued. The opposing argument was that options expensing were a guess, at best. How would you know if the options would ever be "in the money"? Many employees would leave before vesting. Mr. Buffett suggested this was acceptable as, "So what? Estimates pervade accounting" (WaPo letter 7-6-04). My friend, William Donaldson at the SEC, was with Mr. Buffett on this one. It likely requires some accounting gymnastics and effort to get an approximation of what the costs might be. There could be some rearward looking adjustments, too. The firm could hire some consultants and employ the Black-Scholes value model. Perhaps all of that led to some more accurate accounting. For certain, if you have to expense something now, prudent financial management says you will limit it. Thus, fewer employees receive stock options. If there was an intention to limit the lure of accounting manipulation so senior executives wouldn't get rich from stock options, this is not effective; the option grants are more concentrated among them. This is unfortunate; I really like the story of administrative assistants at Microsoft becoming millionaires. Today, the field has reversed. To attract talent at Twitter, it is reported the firm's stock option expense exceeds their actual income (as does LinkedIn). I suspect it is hard to recruit young people to San Francisco with its high cost of living without stock options. More stock options down the organization chart will lessen income inequality.

Qwest for Truth ...and Change

Long before the Qwest scandal, the largest fine levied by the SEC was $10 million against Xerox. Qwest paid $250 million to settle claims against them. I don't understand the logic of punishing shareowners with a fine when the value of their investment has been savaged by events and the threat of bankruptcy. The private securities litigation against Qwest cost $400 million. The law firm led by William Lerach was to collect $98 million of that settlement. It was reported that he personally collected $70 million for his efforts in securing a record $7.2 billion settlement with Enron. (This too, was not enough for Mr. Lerach as he was later jailed for a kickback scheme.) I would expect the total litigation costs at Qwest to be approximately one billion dollars. In my estimation, the primary beneficiaries were *not* shareowners.

KPMG, the accounting firm, was indicted on charges of "cooking up" a phony tax shelter scheme, helping clients avoid $2.5 billion in taxes. The firm agreed to a Deferred Prosecution Agreement, which allowed it to defer receiving a death sentence, assuming they would correct their fraudulent behavior. KPMG agreed to pay a $456 million in fines, restitution, and penalties to the IRS. In this case, 19 individuals were criminally charged. Thirteen of the defendants had their criminal charges dismissed by Federal Judge Lewis A. Kaplan because the government "strong-armed" KPMG into not paying the legal fees of the defendants and violated their constitutional rights. Judge Kaplan maintained that the government's pressure to cut off the legal fees rose to a level of misconduct that: "shocks the conscience." The government prosecutors may have pushed KPMG too hard in the negotiations, holding out the Deferred Prosecution Agreement unless KPMG sided with them and the terms of the Thompson Memorandum. Fearing a death sentence, KPMG had no choice but to deny its employee's legal fees.

Martha Stewart, the self-made "First Lady" of all things domestic, was jailed for her actions regarding insider trading on ImClone stock. Her prosecutor was James Comey, former Director of the FBI. Mr. Comey chose not to charge Ms. Stewart for insider trading. Rather, he charged her with securities fraud by making her claim of innocence, in essence, a propping up of the stock price of her company, Martha Stewart Omnimedia. She was also charged with making false statements to federal officials who were looking into the insider trading charges, which they ultimately did not pursue. The crux of the matter is that Ms. Stewart was prosecuted for, "…having misled people by denying having committed a crime with which she was not charged," as Cato Institute Senior Fellow Alan Reynolds put it (www.quora.com 11-3-2016). Mr. Comey surprised many with his withering criticism of former First Lady, Hillary Clinton's private email server and her handling of classified information, but then elected not to prosecute her. (I wonder what Ms. Stewart thinks about that outcome?)

I do not harbor a grudge against the SEC. I understand their mission is to protect the investing public and they are up against some pretty crafty crooks. They have endured notable lapses. In the Madoff case, Harry Markopolos identified his Ponzi scheme. He went to the SEC to present his case in 2000, 2001, and 2005, which included presenting documents substantiating his claims. He was largely ignored by the SEC staff, which performed only cursory investigations. The Madoff scheme finally collapsed in 2008. Losses sustained by investors totaled $18 billion. Bernard Madoff was sentenced to 150 years in prison.

Similarly, Leyla Wydler who was fired for refusing to participate in the scam called out the Ponzi scheme of Stanford Financial Group. She wrote the SEC in 2003, saying the activity at Stanford

Financial, "…is the subject of a lingering corporate fraud scandal perpetrated as a massive Ponzi scheme that will destroy the life savings of many, damage the reputation of all associated parties, ridicule securities and banking authorities, and shame the United States of America." It wasn't until 2009 that the scam finally fell apart. It was reported that $7 billion of investor money was lost. R. Allen Stanford was sentenced to 110 years in prison.

There have been a number of changes in the approach used by the SEC. Under Chairwoman Mary Jo White the SEC is using an internal administrative judge to decide many cases. This is being vigorously challenged as a due process issue. Additionally, the SEC has adopted a requirement where defendants settling cases no longer have the option to settle the matter "neither admitting nor denying" the allegations, thus requiring an admission of liability. The SEC's budget has grown from $377 million in 2000 to $1.6 billion in 2016. In 2005, the SEC budget was $913 million, and they had 630 enforcement actions. In 2014, the budget was $1.35 billion, and the number of enforcement actions totaled seven hundred and fifty-five. Presumably, this large increase in funding has made the SEC more pervasive and presumably more effective. No individual was jailed for actions related to the housing crash and following Great Recession, although the large banks have paid over $200 billion in assorted fines and penalties. The *Wall Street Journal* reports large sums of the fines collected did not benefit affected homeowners; some of these funds were used for general government purposes.

The implementation of Sarbanes Oxley has been a boon for those in the field of compliance. The law has increased the raw cost of compliance, including director and officers' insurance premiums, increased board costs due to time and liability constraints, software costs, and consulting costs. It has also had the unintended consequence of driving some foreign-domiciled to close shop in the U.S., thereby exporting the problem of poorly governed enterprises (Kellogg). (Becoming a compliance officer is a fast-growing occupation and is growing even faster now with Dodd-Frank financial regulations.)

SOX did not prevent the failure of Lehman Brothers with its quarterly "window dressing" using repo 105's to make its finances look much better than they were. Nor was enough attention paid to the amount of leverage used by Lehman Brothers reported to be on the order of $40 borrowed for every dollar of bank equity. Neither of these types of activities should have been permitted and when Lehman collapsed it mushroomed into the Great Recession.

In current times, companies have lapsed into the practice of using "adjusted" earnings, which is the opposite intent of the push for greater transparency. There are a number of advertisers selling financial products that are better than the "Wall Street casino." The Obama Treasury responded by issuing a U. S. Department of Labor edict that financial advisors need to meet the "fiduciary standard" because novice investors were paying too much for their investment advice and trades. Americans should have confidence in our financial markets. We should all be more educated in how our economy works and the importance of investing for the long term. We seem to have political actors who incite fear and wish to exercise greater control. It is the confluence of limited knowledge of economics and finance coupled with government intervention that worries me about our future.

It is the character of the people who run these companies that matter most. (Perhaps this is another great argument for having more women in senior management roles and on more corporate boards.) The corporate culture that pursues excellence and integrity in its actions is paramount. Management must open itself up to examination, and employees must be encouraged to speak up and have their words be acted upon. Members of the Board of Directors must invest more time to understand the business, and they need to have sufficient independence from management.

There is no amount of rulemaking, regulatory oversight, or compliance actions that will change the nature of man. There is a diminishing return on placing extensive oversight and reporting requirements on business, and I believe we have reached that point today. American business is a cornerstone of our prosperity and all of the benefits that are derived from healthy economic activity. American business provides great satisfaction to its customers, suppliers, employees, and investors. The lack of major scandals in more recent times suggests this era was an anomaly. Let's get back to the business of America, doing business in an unfettered, ethical, and free-market environment with all the glory and risk that entails.

about the author

RICK WESTON spent 20 years in sales, marketing and product development. He was lucky enough to experience major changes in the technology landscape as his career spanned telephony during deregulation, the advent of wireless communication, global fiber optics deployments, the commercialization of the Internet and the power of software. His career was centered in large, well-funded start up companies. His career took him from California to Washington State to Colorado to Tel Aviv and innumerable other stops around the world.

He now makes his home in Georgetown, Texas.

www.ingramcontent.com/pod-product-compliance
Lightning Source LLC
Chambersburg PA
CBHW050540300426
44113CB00012B/2201